"It's an honor to endorse this important and timely book! Doug has not only unpacked valuable relationship concepts and skills in this book but has also modeled the kind of vulnerability that is needed if we want to grow and enjoy more satisfying relationships with our loved ones and colleagues. Doug has helped me grow in my emotional awareness and capacities, and I remain forever grateful for his friendship and example of how to live authentically. Buy the book, read it today! I'm confident you will benefit greatly!"

—LONNIE POWELL, *MBA, telecom consultant*

———

"I've been delighted to get to know Doug over the past few years and watch this book come to fruition. His message about the power of vulnerability is both surprising (How can admitting weakness make me strong?) and life-giving (When I am vulnerable about weakness, I open myself to love in my innermost being). Whether you're a guy who's looking for a refreshing way to become more attractive and effective, or a woman who knows a guy looking for love in all the wrong ways, *Real Men Are Vulnerable* is essential reading."

—CHAD R. ALLEN, *writing coach, founder of BookCamp, author of* Do Your Art

———

"I never finish reading a book. I read Doug's book all the way through and then wondered if it was too short."

—ART CHOKENEA, *International Business Owner*

REAL MEN ARE VULNERABLE

VULNERABLE

REAL MEN ARE

How Emotional Availability Makes Men More Attractive & Effective

DOUG KELLENBERGER

Published by The LeaderCatalyst

ISBN: 979-8-218-55521-4 (Paperback)
ISBN: 979-8-218-55522-1(eBook)

Edited by Chad R. Allen & Lois G. Stück
Cover designed by Mulyana D-Zign
Author photo on back cover by Cheyney Rose
Text design and composition by John Reinhardt Book Design

I dedicate this book...

to my sweet, faithful wife, who loyally supported, stabilized, and stuck with me during her painful years of my emotional immaturity. I'm a better man for being married to her.

And...

to my mother, for her openness about the affection she wished she had given me more of. Her admission at the age of eighty-nine was a genuine gift of love and helped me clarify the origin of my attachment pain.

CONTENTS

Preface xi

Acknowledgements xv

Introduction: Excerpt from My Life 1

1. Why Emotion Is as Necessary as Thought:
   Two Sides to Truth. 5

2. Three Stories of Loss and Redemption. 17

3. Understanding the Journey: *The 5 Stages to Emotional
   Development* 31

4. Beginning: *It's Okay to Not Know How* 45

5. The Paradox of Vulnerability: *How Strength Comes
   through Weakness* 51

6. Grasping a New Paradigm: *Knowing the Kindness
   of God Helps You Let Down Your Guard* 61

7. It's Not Good to Be Alone (Even When God Is with You) . . . 67

8. The Necessity of Receiving: *Instead of Striving
   to Obtain What You Want*. 79

9. The You You've Always Been: *Uncovering the Most
   Attractive and Effective Part of Yourself*. 95

10. Staying Relational: *Even When Life Gets Difficult*. 107

11. Still Mending but Now Together: *The Joy and Strength
    of Emotional Connection*. 121

Endnotes. 129

Preface

THE CONCEPT OF EMOTIONAL CONNECTION is not rocket science, but it is brain science and is now discovered to be the most effective ingredient for enjoyment, emotional health, and life optimization.

This relational concept has been basic to human existence since the beginning of time. But today, in our post-modern, independent world, its usage has greatly diminished. I received little emotional connection as a boy other than the interest and time my grandpa spent with me. As a result I didn't develop emotionally. My predominant interest growing up was in accomplishment. My physical body grew, but my emotional maturity stayed very young and underdeveloped.

Today I understand how a lack of emotional availability hurt my marriage, family, and business interactions.

Women often comment about their boyfriends or husbands: "I just wish he'd grow up!" Or if they address them directly, "Everything is always about you!"

My wife felt the same way. She admitted her own relational difficulty but tried to communicate with me when we were first married. After repeatedly feeling unheard and disregarded, she said she had to stop to protect herself from getting hurt again. She felt like she was married to a boy who was too emotionally underdeveloped to care about anything other than himself.

It has taken me a long time and a lot of emotional pain to learn the importance of relationships. But now having pursued vulnerable interactions with others, I've learned to emotionally connect with people, and it has been the most satisfying and healing experience in my life. It has restored relationships with my wife and family, and it has definitely given me a more authentic and effective way to relate with people.

That's why I'm writing this book. I want the same for you!

A lot of women feel the way my wife did. They nod in agreement when I tell them the title of this book.

Men react differently. They don't like vulnerability. They resist and avoid the topic. Maybe this is natural for the male ego. Maybe it's from a neurobiological difference between men and women. Maybe it's a scheme from the spiritual enemy to undermine relationships. But for sure, our misinformed masculine culture urges men to keep their guard up, stay isolated, remain in control, and do whatever they do without asking for help.

Before completing this book I interviewed men to make sure my topic was relevant. The specific questions I asked were about vulnerability and emotional issues. The following are examples:

- What is your reaction when you hear the title: Real Men Are Vulnerable: How Emotional Availability Makes Men More Attractive and Effective?
- Does being more attractive/enjoyable and effective interest you?
- What does becoming emotionally available mean to you? Is it important? Would you like to learn how to be that?
- What issue(s) do you struggle with the most? If you felt safe to be honest, what physical, mental, emotional, or relational area of life would you like to experience more success in?

Some of their responses were:

- "I hate the word vulnerability!"
- "I don't want to look weak."
- "My favorite chapter is number 4, 'It's Okay to Not Know How.'"
- "I want others to want to be with me. I desire to be desired (more attractive/enjoyable), and I want to be successful (more effective) in life."
- "I feel intrigued and curious about the title of this book."
- "The thing I struggle with the most is being able to be corrected by my angry wife without feeling terrified and bursting into tears like a seven-year-old."

I share these responses to assure you that the same kind of feelings you may be experiencing about this topic exist in other men as well.

The concept, importance, how-to, and rewards of becoming emotionally vulnerable, available, and connected to others is what this book is about.

This is a work of nonfiction, but certain names, places, and other identifying details have been changed to protect the privacy of those involved.

Acknowledgments

I DEEPLY APPRECIATE my grad school director, Dr. Jerry Davis, who "saw me," understood what I valued, and pointed me toward the healing concepts of relationships and emotional connection.

The ideas in this book come from what I have learned from the following people:

Pastor Dick Hostetler, dick@thrivinglife.org
Dr. Jim Wilder, www.lifemodelworks.org
Karl Lehman, M.D., The Immanuel Approach for Emotional Healing and for Life, www.immanuelapproach.com
Heather Forbes, www.beyondconsequences.com
Dr. Bryan Post, www.bryanpost.com

Over the past six years I have been joined, listened to, and accepted by a small group of invaluable guys who have been with me during my dark and despondent times. They and a few other key people have spoken prophetic and encouraging words that have motivated me. They have reminded me to stay vulnerable. They have kept me authentic. And they have gotten me back on track. I remember each one of you and what you have contributed!

Thank you, beta readers, for your time, effort, and input to make this book more relevant and effective.

I appreciate my wife for her honest input, and my kids for sharing their hearts, key ideas, and encouragement.

Finally, I never would have completed this book without my writing coach, Chad R. Allen. He helped me structure the book and edit my wording, and he guided me through the publication process. He also connected emotionally with me throughout the process, encouraged me, and gave me great, insightful advice based on his many years of experience.

Thank you, Chad!

Introduction
Excerpt from My Life

ANGER AND DESPERATION compelled me to make it to my therapy session that afternoon. Several interruptions gave me an excuse to cancel. But I didn't. I couldn't.

I didn't want to go through this pain anymore. And I couldn't keep doing it alone. I needed help. My emotional rage was way out of control.

Most people didn't know this about me. I was an ordained minister and a licensed mental health counselor. My heart was sincere, and in public I kept my composure, but in private, when no one was around, this rageful anger would sneak up out of nowhere and express itself verbally. The smallest thing set me off—dropping my keys, bumping my head, getting an automated customer service recording that wouldn't let me speak to a real person.

It happened whenever my unprocessed feelings of being disregarded as a child got triggered again. Any unwanted response that got filtered to me as "I don't care how you feel!" would send me into this cursing rage.

It felt embarrassing to admit at my age. I thought I should have been more mature by now and have better control over this. But no matter how hard I tried, how much I prayed, or how sincere I was, nothing changed. That's because up until this turning point, I did everything alone and relied very little on anyone else.

A good friend and sales buddy used to say, "I want to be a part of a team." His relational ability made him effective with customers, and that's the collaborative interaction he wanted with our sales team. But this always felt "wussy" to me. Doing something by myself felt stronger. "All I need is God" was my mantra. But in reality, this was just an excuse to keep myself isolated from people so I wouldn't get hurt.

For a long time it felt safer to operate alone, but that never helped me get better.

I woke up in a bad mood on the day of my appointment. It progressed into a consuming anger and then cursing at God. I had been in this dark, negative place before, but never to this degree. It felt unbearable. I wanted to die. I was too tired to go through it again, and I just wanted it to end. I actually prayed for that to happen but wasn't convinced my final resting place would be any better. So I surrendered and went to the appointment.

There, in that angry, cursing pain, my relational mentor, Pastor Dick Hostetler, and I started our session. I shared some thoughts but mostly my feelings. I didn't know if what I described was in the right chronological order. I just knew I had to talk with someone and get relief. He asked a few clarifying questions, but mostly he listened. It felt good to experience someone with me. Nothing got resolved that day, but at least I didn't feel alone.

From there—and in continued sessions—the emotional processing led to a greater awareness of where my pain was coming from, what I had been doing unsuccessfully to try and get rid of it, and how that effort was actually covering up my true self and what it was longing for.

And I can draw an unbroken line from that first session to the book you're holding. I hope it encourages you to put your protective guard down; find a trusted person and then a community to interact with; let yourself begin to develop emotionally by receiving acceptance, validation, and affirmation from others, which is what your heart is actually crying out for.

I've experienced it, and neuroscience now proves it. The human brain operates best when it feels emotionally connected with another brain—when we feel seen, known, and enjoyed by another person.

And that is what I want for you!

The good news is that you won't have to try harder or be better to do it. Your brain is already wired for it. All you have to do is cooperate with it.

This book will take you on a step-by-step journey to do that. You will discover:

- the emotional connection your heart is desiring,
- how being vulnerable helps you get it,
- what happens without it,
- a non-threatening place to start,
- a new perspective to motivate you,
- the link between childhood wounds and sabotaging behavior that prevents you from connecting with someone in a satisfying way,
- your unique identity,
- the effectiveness of a relational approach that will surprise you.

Ready to start? You may feel some hesitation. I certainly did, and still do sometimes, but I know it's the only thing that works. For me it began by opening up myself to another person.

That's how it will begin for you...

For a long time it felt safer to operate alone,
but that never helped me get better.

Why Emotion Is as Necessary as Thought
Two Sides to Truth

THE DARK AND EMPTY FEELING overwhelmed me in that first session. Something was crying out from within, and I was tired of holding it back in favor of what everyone else wanted me to say.

I hoped my mentor was safe. I knew him to be an emotionally mature minister who was experienced in connecting with traumatized people. I kept checking his expression, watching for any reaction that indicated he was judging me. Because at this point, I didn't know what would come out of my mouth.

It's a blur now, but I recall snorting cuss words at God.

It wasn't my true heart's expression. It was a reaction to pain—from a strong emotional part of me that I hadn't yet understood.

We've all been there—expressing ourselves irrationally in ways that we hadn't yet defined—trying to convey something important without knowing what it was.

As you read on you'll learn the necessity of connecting with and then processing this emotional part of yourself with another person to obtain clarity and release from it.

Two Sides

You know what they say: "There are two sides to every story!" That's how it is inside our brain: there's the thinking side and the emotional side. Each side has its own perspective, and they often don't agree!

Take, for example, the following conflicting perspectives:

The COVID quarantine provided time to write, but this empty ache distracted me to binge watch movies.

God's word says He'll never leave me, but this despairing depression makes me feel alone and want my life to end.

I know being honest is the right thing to do, but I'm scared I'll get yelled at if I do.

I need to ask for help, but doing that makes me feel shamefully inadequate, and I'm afraid I'll lose control of what I want if I involve other people in the process.

Our feelings can't be ignored regardless of how true we believe our thoughts to be.

For most of my life I experienced a recurring pattern of starting something and then losing interest and quitting. I tried to overcome this pattern by thinking positive thoughts—like the Bible verse, "I can do all things through Christ who strengthens me" (Philippians 4:13 NKJV). But an empty and inadequate feeling would overcome me, and I'd stop anyway.

Thinking true thoughts is important, but often, if we want to change a behavior, something deeper needs to be felt in the emotional side of our brain to give us the motivation to *want* to do it. If this doesn't happen, our most determined willpower will be overridden by a resistance that causes us to either shut down or act out in a sabotaging way that our reasoning mind won't be able to stop.

No neural path exists from the thinking part of our brain to directly regulate the emotional part of our brain. You can't just intellectually tell an out-of-control emotion to stop. Have you ever tried to use reasoning to console a terrified and hysterical child or a suicidal person? It doesn't work. Something emotional has to connect with the emotional part of an experience to regulate its reaction.

Sharon Kuhn, in her book *Empathy: A Guide to Maximizing Human Potential*, explains the "coregulating" power of an emotional connection with a person who understands how we feel and is willing to join and "empathize" with us in whatever we're going through.[1] This emotional joining fills an empty gap. It calms us. It produces an internal energy that conveys: I'm not alone; someone is with me who cares; I feel accepted and wanted regardless of my shortcomings.

My heart goes out to the well-meaning spiritual leaders who have succumbed to damaging sexual behavior that marred their reputation and ministry. Their gifting included exceptional knowledge and leadership skills, but I know from experience, if their approach didn't include the necessity of experiencing enjoyable and validating connections with people, it wouldn't be enough to satisfy the unfulfilled gap that the emotional side of their brain was longing for. And as is so often the case, addictions develop in this space to make up for the emotional satisfaction that is missing.

As you'll learn in chapter 7, the antidote for addiction is connection—not abstinence and sobriety.

> *No neural path exists from the thinking part of our brain to directly regulate the emotional part of our brain. Only an emotional connection can do that.*

How the Brain Works

In the last thirty years neuroscience has shown that brains operate at their best when they experience enjoyable emotional connection (or the memory of one) with another brain.

Drs. Marcus Warner and Jim Wilder emphasize this point in their book *Rare Leadership*: "Our deepest need and most desperate craving is joyful relationships." "Joy is…the most desirable and powerful of motivating factors in our lives." "Every time people are glad to be together and withstand adversity, their joy-strength grows, and their emotional capacity becomes greater."[2] (Scripture emphasizes the same point when it says, "The Joy of the LORD is our strength," Nehemiah 8:10 NKJV.)

In a later book, Wilder and Warner cite the validity of this brain science "based on research coming out of the UCLA Medical Center and the work of brain science experts like Allan Schore, and Daniel Siegel, Iain McGilchrist, and others."[3]

In embryo and early childhood the emotional side of the brain develops first. The ability to analyze, problem solve, and speak develops later. Neurological impulses travel through the brain in the same sequence. Emotion is experienced first in our brain before thought is realized.

Wilder and Warner describe emotional reaction as the "fast-track"[4] of the brain because it happens quicker than the slower rational side of our thinking. That's how we're able to jump out of the way of a bus or duck a punch without having to analyze it first.

This faster reacting, emotional side of the brain is what often drives our behavior—a lot of times without us being conscious of it. Healthy and optimal behavior then depends on the maturity of this emotional part of the brain. And this maturation can only happen with emotional connection between people.

Let's see why!

The emotional right brain operates from bottom to top. And Dr. Wilder, in his book *The Complete Guide to Living with Men*, uses this bottom to top progression to explain how emotional connection is necessary to develop maturity. He says the top executive level of our emotional brain—the one that regulates emotion and helps us act like our true self—only "stays on as long as the Emotional Connection level just below it can stay synchronized."[5] The synchronization he's talking about is the enjoyable emotional connection people make when they relate with each other. Warner and Wilder write, "From bottom to top the right brain is designed to seek, build, and thrive on joyful relationships."[6]

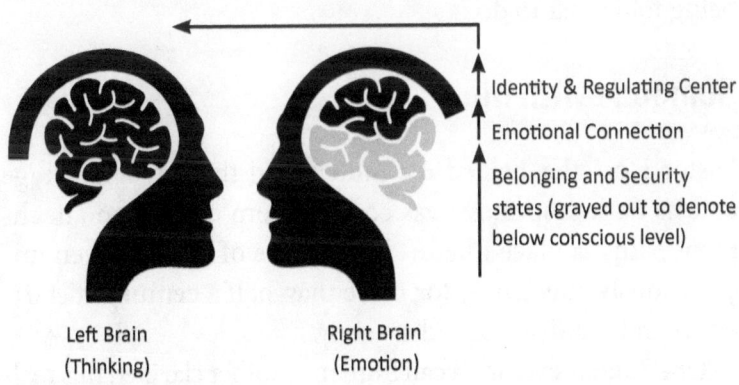

Left Brain
(Thinking)

Right Brain
(Emotion)

Identity & Regulating Center

Emotional Connection

Belonging and Security
states (grayed out to denote
below conscious level)

The right emotional side of the brain reacts before the thinking side of the brain and operates from its bottom level to the top. Therefore: the top level that regulates our emotions and helps us act like ourselves only stays operating as long as the Emotional Connection level below it feels attuned to and validated by another brain.

Our brain operates at its best when it experiences an emotional connection (or the memory of one) with another brain.

That's why small groups who emotionally connect produce more growth and maturity than someone who just listens to good informational sermons.

My wife used to say, "Stop trying to fix me and just listen!" She wanted to feel cared about and understood before hearing my advice about what I thought she should do.

Dr. Wilder says an upset and overwhelmed brain needs emotional connection from another brain to calm down and act like it's true self. Without this coregulating synchronization, an upset and overwhelmed person goes into survival mode to make the distress go away—resulting in either irrational behavior, self-medication, running away, or shutting down.

That's why my wife wanted to feel listened to instead of being told what to do.

Someone with Me

Pastor Hostetler helped me understand that my angry rage and its dark emptiness was coming from childhood attachment pain—a place I hadn't been aware of but had been unconsciously affected by for more than half a century. It started when I felt disregarded as a boy.

One Sunday evening a call from my mother clarified this realization: "Douglas!" she said, "This morning in church I noticed all the young mothers affectionately loving and kissing on their babies during the service and realized I never did that to you when you were a little boy!" And then with tears I could hear through her voice, "I wish you were a baby again so I could!"

I was stunned for a long time after we hung up, but appreciative—and still am—that my eighty-nine-year-old mother would humbly express what I had unconsciously felt for decades but couldn't put into words. Her honorable admission validated a big piece of my childhood story. And it's for this reason that she is one of the people to whom I dedicate this book.

As a result of this attachment pain, I developed compensating behaviors to minimize my distress; and up until recent years, I had been continuing to operate in them:

- pleasing and performing to get approval
- achieving to feel valuable
- isolating myself for protection
- exerting myself to earn acceptance
- fantasizing to escape the pain

Since 2018 my wife's autoimmune disease progressed to the point of requiring my presence to provide 24/7 care for her at home. This restriction took some of my compensating options away, and the need to stay focused on her caused me to face the long-standing difficulty we had in connecting with each other. The whole situation was one of those God-arranged circumstances that forced me to work on myself. I could no longer escape or avoid it. I had no other choice but to process my attachment pain. It was probably the first time in life I was ready.

That's what Pastor Hostetler and I did in our sessions—processed the painful root of my rageful behavior.

The cursing and yelling at God seemed to increase with every rageful outburst. The reasoning, thinking side of my brain—the part that had been religiously trained—expected punishment from God for expressing myself like that to Him. It didn't happen. I'm glad because I couldn't help it. In an instant, pressure would build up and explode inside my head. I would apologize profusely to Him every time it happened, but I always knew deep down that I'd do it again. And whenever I did, God just patiently and without condemnation hung in there with me.

Pastor Hostetler did the same thing. He sat and listened with no judgment, no lecture about how a child of God should talk differently. In fact, he has written a book titled *The Emotional Jesus*. In it he explains, "I'm learning it is far more important to be emotionally present with someone in despair than to try to rescue him or her from the bad feelings."[7] It didn't matter to him what words I used. He said he was more concerned about the deep pain I was experiencing and wanted to be with me in it so I wouldn't feel alone.

And evidently, that's what God must have been doing all those times I cursed at Him.

> *It is far more important to be emotionally present with someone in their despair than to try to rescue (or correct) them in their bad feelings.*

Emotional connection is not a complicated endeavor, but it takes intention and practice. It can be experienced with anyone who has empathy, wants to understand, and values relationship.

To illustrate the power of feeling heard, connected with, and validated, let me share a few examples from my own life.

Acceptance and Validation

I woke up one Sunday morning feeling depressed. I tried to enjoy a new cigar, but it made me feel dizzy. My mind flipped through its typical fantasies in an attempt to escape from the pain, but that felt uncomfortable and betraying. Going to church was a usual routine, but the effort of getting there, putting on my game face, and giving the usual "I'm fine" responses felt like too much work.

That's when I remembered the conversation I had earlier with my son. I had expressed regret for not being there for him emotionally when he was a boy, and he listened with acceptance and then expressed his feelings back to me. It felt good to be honest and then feel his reciprocating love and appreciation. Remembering this enjoyment made me feel better.

Another example includes an interaction with my first sales manager thirty-eight years ago. He went with me to look at a dump truck I was considering for my side landscaping business. He really didn't care about the truck or the landscaping business. He preferred that I'd sell more sofas and chairs. But his interest in me showed that he cared. I still remember appreciating that. It made me want to sell more furniture for him.

A European friend recently emailed about an enjoyable memory she experienced when visiting our home. She wrote, "The other day I was remembering how we were at your place, sitting around your table (with the gum-ball machine on it). I was telling you about my job and you were so genuinely interested. I enjoyed that so much!"

One more example comes to mind. Each month I had been meeting with a group of men to process our emotions. We focused on sharing feelings because that's the pathway to

experience satisfying connection. One morning I felt empty, depleted, and didn't even want to be there. This emotion
shifted when one of the guys expressed anger and resentment
toward his boss for not recognizing him. I related with that
feeling. His vulnerability validated something real inside of
me, and it made me come alive. The emotional processing
ended up as an encouragement to everyone in the group.

*Sharing feelings... (is) the pathway
to experience satisfying connection.*

What the Bible Says about Emotions

A lot of people make the assumption that Proverbs 23:7 only
says, "For as [a man] thinks . . . so is he" (NKJV). But the
complete verse states, "As [a man] thinks *in his heart*..." The
"thinking" that determines who we become includes the
emotional side of our brain.

God also emphasizes the role of emotion in the salvation
verse, "*With the heart* one believes unto righteousness" (Romans 10:10 NKJV).

I believe *mind renewal* referred to in Romans 12:2 takes
place in our whole brain—including both the thinking and
emotional sides.

How Jesus's Brain Worked

As we close this chapter, let's look at how these principles
played out in the life of God Himself.

Jesus used emotional connection to protect and effectively
influence a woman caught in adultery (John 8:3–11). When
intensely pressured to respond to the deceitful manipulation

of the adulteress's accusers, Jesus didn't defend Himself. He was more concerned about protecting the shamefully exposed woman, so He stooped down and wrote in the dust to divert attention away from her.

He didn't answer the religious leader's accusation with a rational argument. He emotionally disarmed their aggression by joining them in their assessment of her behavior. He then exposed their hypocrisy by switching the focus from religious legality to emotional awareness by asking the one who never sinned to throw the first stone.

When the threat against her was gone, the woman felt safe enough to begin interacting with Jesus by answering His question. When she finally realized that He didn't condemn her, the woman's defenses dropped, and it was in this moment that she became the most receptive to hear His directive (which He had wisely withheld until this point) to go and sin no more.

Our culture recognizes the accumulation of knowledge and the ability to effectively strategize as some of its highest forms of human capability. But in reality, we are much more appreciated, attractive to others, and far more effective in life when we learn how to connect emotionally with ourselves and those with whom we interact.

We are much more appreciated, attractive to others, and far more effective in life when we learn how to connect emotionally.

Three Stories of Loss and Redemption 2

IN THE LAST CHAPTER I explained how emotional connection is essential to optimize our mental health and create our most enjoyable relationships.

In this chapter I share stories from my own life about what happened when emotional connection didn't exist in my marriage, family, and business interactions, and how that became redeemed.

Story #1: Married to a Boy

"I just wish he'd grow up," is a quote in the preface that refers to the emotional level of maturity a majority of men find themselves in:

- not aware of how they feel and how it affects their behavior
- not aware of how their partner, child, or business associates feel
- uncomfortable talking about feelings
- reluctant to ask for help to find out
- unable to remain relational when they get upset
- defending themselves and blaming others instead of taking responsibility

Emotionally underdeveloped men can have good intentions and often great imaginations about what they want for their marriage, being a father, and sometimes for their lives. But when life gets too stressful, they don't (and neither did I) have enough emotional capacity to withstand the difficulty long enough to follow through on their intentions. They get afraid, lash out in anger, or check out to get away from the pressure.

Eventually a woman who is in a relationship with an emotionally underdeveloped man realizes she can't trust that he'll "be there" for her, so she ends up (even inadvertently) distancing herself from relying on him and instead seeks ways, on her own, to take care of herself and the needs of her children.

Remembering the Fear

My wife patiently waited until I finished helping her with night-time preparations before she answered my request.

I had asked if she would delight (emotionally) in me. It felt vulnerable and scary to do, but I was practicing a child-level maturity task of asking for something I wanted—what I had been learning to do in my emotional processing group and a weekly relationship class.[8]

She didn't respond emotionally with the sparkling joy in her eyes that I hoped for. But it was with a heartfelt appreciation of all the care I had been giving her and the work I had been doing on her behalf around the house.

And it meant a lot to me...but then with red, teary eyes she painfully started reflecting on an earlier time in our marriage when she seriously questioned if I would ever be there *for her* if she needed my help.

I knew why.

Married life back then was all about me. It wasn't that I didn't care about her. I just didn't have the emotional capacity to empathize with her (or with anyone). I didn't know how. My limited capacity was still focused on accomplishments to get what I wanted. Even my decision to ask her to marry me was more about achieving a successful obedience to God than relationally accepting and enjoying the gift of her companionship He had given me.

"When I first married Doug, it felt right," my wife said, "like God wanted me to. And I thought it would be my opportunity to feel important to someone. But that didn't happen. I tried to share how I felt, but I didn't feel listened to or understood. I came to understand that the only room he had in his head was space for himself."

"We'd make plans and he'd change them without telling me. If something came up, I always felt pressured to comply with the change. It was hard for him to not to get what he wanted. And if he didn't get it, he would become moody and give me the silent treatment."

"It seemed like he expected me to make him happy—like he wanted me to be his mother. . . . It felt like I was married to a boy."

It's no wonder she questioned that night about whether I'd *be there* for her someday.

She Didn't Feel Seen

I distinctly remember how feminine and captivating her arms swayed back and forth as my pregnant wife ambled up the sidewalk of our college campus to meet me for a class I asked her to attend. An acknowledgement of her beauty would have been a wonderful way to let her know that I noticed her! I'm sure she wasn't excited about attending this class with a bunch of strangers, so that acknowledgement would have been appreciated for the loyal effort she extended to support me. Unfortunately *telling her this* never crossed my mind; nor would I have had the courage to do it.

There are photographs of her natural beauty I look back on now that catch my breath. But then my underdeveloped maturity wasn't able to see it. The only neural pathways I had in my brain of viewing women were ones formed in teenage years from lusting after sexy Playboy Bunnies and the glamorized females I'd watch being kissed in romance movies.

She Couldn't Trust Me

My wife described a distressing incident on our honeymoon: "I was scared when he took the canoe out after dark. The cabin rules prohibited that. But when I expressed my fear, he ignored me and did it anyway."

And there were other memories: "We were supposed to be a team at the mission we worked at, but I never felt included. He'd busy himself with activity, but none of it felt connected with me."

"He wouldn't follow through on decisions we'd make about disciplining the kids. He'd end up taking their side. And I was left feeling alone and hurt."

"I learned I couldn't trust him."

"When he broke an important vase that was gifted to me, he glued it back together and hid it behind the end table. When I asked why he didn't tell me, he said, 'I was afraid you'd get mad.' He was more concerned about protecting his feelings than caring about how hurt I felt."

"Financial stewardship was important to me. But he would borrow more money than we agreed on. He bought a new van against my advice that forced a near foreclosure on our home. Nothing I said made a difference to him."

I learned I couldn't trust him.

I did have good characteristics that my wife valued. She said she knew, even before we were married, that I was devoted to God and wanted to live for Him. Those were qualities that attracted her to me. But she didn't realize how emotionally immature I was and how self-absorbed my attempts were to still get my own unresolved needs met.

I didn't know it either—how that emotional immaturity would sabotage my sincere spiritual intentions and end up hurting her.

Second Savior

Faithful wives have an extraordinary capacity to put up with a lot of hurt, neglect, and emotional abuse. I think they've been divinely equipped that way to function as (what I refer to) a "second savior" for the emotional and character development of their man—if their man will allow that to happen. But there comes a time when a woman's sincere attempts to be loyal and committed get so hurt and so painfully disregarded that her resolve snaps, like an overstretched rubber band, into little fragments that seem impossible to put back together again.

There came a time like that for my wife. She didn't divorce me, but she gave up trying to get my attention and ended up "leaving" me emotionally. She said she had to. The hurt of feeling unimportant and unaccepted was too much to continue bearing.

How It Turned Out

The responsibility of caring for my wife in these later years and the willingness to work on my attachment pain (instead of running from it) forced me to ask for help and be willing

21

to interact vulnerably in relationships in order to allow my maturity to grow.

Tonight, as I sat patiently on the edge of my wife's bed, I was able to understand and empathize with her past pain and the fearful insecurity she felt back then of not knowing whether I would "be there" for her someday.

And the difference in my reaction, tonight, was a far cry from how it had been in the past.

I began rehearsing to her out loud what I would have done then, knowing what I do now, about joining and validating her so she would have felt understood, cared about, and not alone.

I realized more than ever how tender, quiet, and compliant her personality was. My mind flashed back to a serene image of her cutting the cake with me in our wedding photo. And I wished that I would have better known then how to hold and console her later that evening when she complained of a stomachache.

I gently stroked my hand across her cheek and brushed lightly across her hair to let her know that this is how I would have done it.

Words of love weren't necessary that evening when we said goodnight. The appreciation in her moist eyes and the extra grip on my hand that didn't want to let go said it all.

Story #2: Fathered by a Boy

I always felt closer to my kids when I was away on sales trips. I'd think of them often, enjoyed talking with them on the car phone, and excitedly brought back little gifts ("prizes" we used to call them) from wherever I'd been.

But when I got home, I'd retreat off by myself, into my office, or go out and work on something alone—someplace that separated me from the pressure of feeling responsible for what they needed. It wasn't that I didn't care about them; I just didn't have the capacity to engage in the emotion of what they were going through. What little I did have emotionally was unconsciously still being used up trying to get my own unmet childhood needs satisfied. Any demand beyond that felt like an emotional overload that threatened to shut me down or burn me out—like the fear of knowing what would happen if I tried to run the demands of a 220-volt air conditioner on a 110-volt circuit.

The easiest way to deal with this stress was to get away and hide. Isolation was the most expedient way to do that.

> *It wasn't that I didn't care about them; I just didn't*
> *have the capacity to engage in the emotion of what*
> *they were going through.*

Fear and Punishment

My kids ran upstairs when they saw me pull into the driveway after a long sales trip. On one occasion my son said he quickly jumped in back of some bushes. He saw me coming and mentally ran down the checklist of the jobs I had given him. When he realized he had forgotten one, he panicked and ducked behind the shrub.

When I was away on sales trips my wife set a gentle and quiet rhythm in the house. Sometimes she'd get distracted, but the kids always knew she was safe. When I came home, all that was disrupted. She said, "You'd come in the door and immediately start telling everyone what to do." Security for me came from feeling in control, and satisfaction came from getting a lot done. I had little awareness of the benefit of relationships. If I wanted something accomplished or wanted to train the kids "in the way [they] should go" (Proverbs 22:6 ESV), I used fear and punishment.

Now I understand why they all ran upstairs when I pulled into the driveway.

They All Left When I Was Appointed

My adult children eventually left the church we attended after I was appointed an elder. The position was honoring to me, something that made me feel significant, and a role I had always wanted. I did take it seriously and tried my sincerest to do a good job, but the lack of maturity and consideration I displayed toward my kids and their mother at home wasn't consistent with the character of that office. They knew how I became angry and "checked out" when emotional pressure built up. And they didn't feel confident I'd make decisions in their best interest when a church situation arose that would be threatening to my own needs. My daughter tried to explain this to me, but I ignored it and accepted the position anyway.

I had the talents of a leader but lacked the emotional maturity. A friend tried to explain how much more important it would be if I'd spend time nurturing my son instead of chasing after my own dreams. I heard his words. The rational part of my brain understood the logic, but the emotional part of my brain that was still hurt and underdeveloped couldn't stop its unconscious, preoccupied drive to perform and achieve to satisfy my unmet needs.

I Couldn't Receive

My family was offered an all-expense-paid vacation with another family to the NASA Space Station in Huntsville, Alabama. My kids would have loved it, but I said no!

"We're not going," I told my wife. I couldn't accept the offer. My shame wouldn't let me. I understood why the family offered this. They knew how strapped for money we were. A lot of church people knew. Once we found a hundred-dollar bill in our mailbox. Another time someone purchased meat for us at the local grocery store and called to say it was there for pick up.

I didn't want to feel dependent on others. In my mind only *I* had to be the one who fixed our financial situation.

I felt angry! Actually, underneath I felt embarrassed about my inadequacy. I hadn't developed the emotional ability to be aware of and process the real issue, so the bottled-up shame exploded into an angry outburst.

"No!" I told my wife. "We are not going to Huntsville!"

My underdeveloped emotions were stuck in shame and an inability to receive, so my kids missed out on a fun vacation.

I hadn't developed the emotional capacity to be aware of and process the real issue, so the bottled-up shame exploded into an angry outburst.

A Clarification

I share many of my failures in this book. This is not intended as a self-deprecating penance for all the mistakes I've made. I did a lot of things right as a father and am proud of that. My kids often bring up what they appreciated about me. Rather, I share these stories to provide numerous and varied examples of what immaturity looks like in men. And in doing so I hope men will see themselves in these examples and be encouraged to do something about their emotional development.

The Gap and Hurt from the Absence of Emotional Connection

A lack of emotional connection between loved ones not only creates an unfulfilled gap in their heart but sends an unconscious message of: "I don't care how you feel; I'm not interested in finding out; and I have other priorities that are more important than you."

Time alone *does not* heal those kind of wounds. Left undealt with, the dissatisfaction of this gap continues to fester.

It's tragic to realize that I *did* care back then, even though I couldn't emotionally connect. But my automatic, defensive, protective, and controlling reactions from undealt-with childhood pain overrode my ability to express that care.

At one point some of my kids wouldn't let me hug them. They didn't trust me either—perhaps they thought my attempts were just more manipulation to get what I wanted. They were trying to grow up and understand who they were. They needed a protective dad to notice and delight in them so they could let their guard down to discover themselves.

There is a counterintuitive but encouraging aspect about emotional connection: You don't have to agree with someone to connect emotionally with them. All you have to do is "see" where they're at emotionally and join them in it. "Rejoice with those who rejoice, and weep with those who weep" (Romans 12:15 NKJV)—regardless of your understanding about what happened or agreement with them.

> *You don't have to agree with someone*
> *to connect emotionally with them.*

Feeling understood calms an upset feeling and experiencing validation satisfies an empty place in the heart. It's amazing how feeling understood and validated by someone endears them to you. This ability to be emotionally available is the quality that makes us more attractive to others.

Becoming emotionally available instead of controlling and isolating must have been what attracted the kids back to me. They sensed I wanted to be with and join them.

We've come a long way.

Now we spend a lot more time together, especially for holidays and birthday celebrations. And we hug! One of our daughters, her husband, and her kids spend their Friday family nights visiting us at my wife's nursing home. I attend workout sessions with my sons. We enjoy time together and watching movies. And this most recent Christmas, even though most of the kids lived within twelve minutes of our house, many of them spent the night to eat and play games.

I've apologized for the past and we've had some good talks, but I think the biggest improvement is me just listening to and enjoying interacting with them.

It's worked with the grandkids too! They say my listening helps them work out whatever they're going through.

Story #3: The Loss of Two Businesses

My landscape business grew to the point of needing someone to help with installations. The person I hired was a welcomed and necessary addition. He enjoyed the work and was knowledgeable. He was trustworthy, hard-working, and amazingly resourceful. But I had difficulty giving up control to let him fully take over that part of the operation. My wife pointed out that we could increase our income if he was allowed to do that so I could concentrate on selling more jobs. She was right, but my undealt-with insecurity and subsequent need for control wouldn't let me.

As a result the landscaping business failed, and I had to do something else.

This controlling pattern repeated itself when I tried to start a counseling business after completing grad school. My fear of inadequacy and collaborating with others made me feel safer staying isolated, so I started a private practice. (These were unresolved issues that limited my competency as a therapist.) I served a few clients a week, had some satisfying sessions, and in my own limited scope saw God's provision; but the business didn't thrive. When I expressed discouragement to a good friend, he said, "Doug, *you're all alone*! You need to be with a group of people who love and value you, so you feel supported."

It was difficult, terrifying actually, to give up control, but I listened to him and went to work with a group of therapists at a counseling agency. It worked. I was loved, validated, and supported by a lot of wonderful, competent people. I enjoyed five successful years there with a full client load. The owner even recognized my aspirations, provided me with affirmation, and eventually helped me launch out in my own direction. I needed to do more inner emotional processing, but working with this group of people was a good start.

Connecting emotionally with the concerns and perspectives of your employees, customers, and staff is also necessary to make your business thrive.

Author of multiple bestselling business books, Patrick Lencioni explains the importance of vulnerable connection for not only "deep and lasting relationships in life" but to obtain a "competitive advantage" in business "for those who embrace it." He wrote, "Vulnerability. It is one of the most undervalued and misunderstood of all human qualities." In his book *Getting Naked: A Business Fable about Shedding the Three Fears that Sabotage Client Loyalty*, Lencioni says this "naked" service, as he calls it, of "honesty, humility, and self-lessness" will:

- "endear" customers to you
- "allow them to trust and depend" on you
- "build stronger, stickier relationships"
- get "those clients to actively and enthusiastically recommend and endorse" you
- allow "more comfortable and collaborative discussions about pricing and fees"
- put you "in a position to more effectively help clients"

At the end of the book Lencioni writes, "There is nothing more attractive and admirable than people who willingly and cheerfully set their egos aside and make the needs of others more important than their own."[9]

Something to Consider

- When someone expresses a concern about what you are doing, try this: instead of immediately going into a defensive, self-justifying mode, take a moment to consider what they are trying to say.
- Do you have a safe, healthy community to process what others are saying about you?
- The next time you feel critical of someone's behavior, try to become aware of the emotions underlying your response.
- Or consider the emotion that might be underlying their behavior.

- If you have a staff retention problem, consider the emotional reasons underlying that.

The need to connect vulnerably with those we love and work with is huge. Emotional connection is the effective process that makes people feel seen, valued, and understood.

It makes all the difference between loss and redemption.

Understanding the Journey
The 5 Stages of Emotional Development

3

BEING EMOTIONALLY UNDERDEVELOPED and unavailable to others doesn't mean you are bad! It has nothing to do with your worth as a person, your value to God, your calling, or your worth to another person who wants to have a relationship with you.

It simply means you are not emotionally developed, and you are not able to connect emotionally with people.

For example:

- You don't know how you feel.
- You have difficulty describing feelings.
- You are uncomfortable talking about feelings.
- You don't know how another person feels and don't know how to connect with them to find out.
- You just want whatever isn't working to be fixed or make whatever feels uncomfortable to go away.

Continuing like this is not going to make you a person to whom others are attracted, and it's not going to make you effective in the relationships you are already in. But acknowledging this undesirable condition and wanting to do something about it is the first step to change. It's the place where you have to start. I call it Ground Zero.

Ground Zero

This is where you know something is wrong. You don't know what it is, but you want it to change.

You may feel dissatisfaction:

- You've worked hard and achieved success but still feel empty.
- You've witnessed a tender wedding ceremony and realized something is missing in your marriage.
- You've attended a funeral and wonder how people will remember you.
- You've watched a couple kiss at the end of a Hallmark movie and longingly wish you could experience that feeling.

You may feel desperation:

- You still love the woman who divorced you, but don't fully understand why she left; and you don't have any idea how you could get her back.
- Your teenage daughter is distraught. You sense she wants something from you, but you have no idea what it is.
- Your son is angry because he doesn't feel understood. He says there's never any consolation talking with you. You want to help him but all your "good advice," Bible verses, and attempts to fix his problems go unappreciated.

You may feel hopeless:

- Your sincere intentions don't produce the results you hoped for.
- Your business idea is great, but its execution fails.
- You want to heal people, but no one is interested in letting you.
- You've attended a lot of leadership seminars, but no one follows you.
- All the effort you've exerted to please God hasn't made you feel closer to Him.

And while you feel dissatisfied, desperate, and hopeless, there is still a willingness to try something different if you knew what it was.

That's what this vulnerable relational approach to emotional development is about—five progressive stages to make you more emotionally available, desirable to be with, and effective in your interactions with others.

These stages include:

1. Discovery of your feelings.
2. Discovery of how others feel.
3. Feeling validated and understood when you talk about your feelings.
4. The formation of a new, redeemed narrative about your life.
5. The ability to emotionally connect with others and experience a more enjoyable and satisfying relationship with them.

You may feel resistant to this relational approach at first. I did. For a long time the fear of getting hurt made me distance myself from experiencing the connections I needed.

Today I'm glad I risked taking this relational journey. It's made the most healing and life-giving difference in my life.

But it is important to understand that emotional development is something that has to be experienced. It can't be obtained by gaining more knowledge or by just reading this book. It can only happen in vulnerable, relational interactions with people.

> *Emotional development is something*
> *that has to be experienced.*

So that's where we begin!

5 Progressive Stages to Emotional Development

1. Share to Become Aware

My friend motioned me to the back of the church. He said he was in a lot of emotional pain and didn't know why. His admission was a surprise because he had always been such a strong and supportive friend to me—he was my first sponsor in the church-based recovery program we were involved in.

Now *he* was asking for help.

He'd been physically sober for a number of years but had never understood the root causes underlying his addiction and had never processed them. Sharing his feelings increased his awareness of those issues. Our interaction gave him access to my resources and encouraging support, and it eventually led him to discover an emotional process of identifying underlying feelings and releasing their pain.

Sharing difficulties with someone and asking for their help will result in the same awareness development for you.

Sometimes in conversations about difficulties I'll get clarity about a problem before finishing my sentence. Dr. Karl Lehman, in his book *The Immanuel Approach: For Emotional Healing and Life*, explains how describing all our thoughts and feelings out loud to someone can have that clarifying effect on our understanding.[10]

And even moderate attempts to share emotions with someone makes our brain more receptive to reveal deeper issues.

I remember the first time I felt lonely at the age of fifty-four. Actually I initially remember it as a feeling of emptiness that surprised me because it happened during my favorite Christmas holiday, and one of our adult children and enjoyable grandchildren were staying with us. I attribute this awareness to group sharing sessions I was required to take in my counseling grad school program. Sharing emotions in that group evidently sensitized me to some deeper, longstanding attachment pain that I had buried since childhood. That sharing not only increased my self-awareness, it also made me receptive to an especially warm greeting from a neighbor that Christmas at our local gas station. That enjoyable and appreciated experience surprised me too!

Sharing feelings not only increases self-awareness but also opens our receptivity to important, helpful, and necessary perspectives from other people. Dr. Karl Lehman, in his book *Outsmarting Yourself*, describes the necessity of receiving accurate input from other sources to ensure accurate "extrapolations" that need to be made in the blind spots of our own retinas.[11]

Accurate input from honest and well-informed feedback produces our best decisions.

My favorite scene in the movie *A Beautiful Mind* takes place when Professor John Nash turns to a colleague and asks, "Was that a real person?" after experiencing someone invite him to a Nobel Prize Induction Ceremony. He had learned to accept the deficiencies of his schizophrenia and knew he needed help from others to make sure he wasn't hallucinating. With a willingness to ask for help, he went on to receive the Nobel Prize in Economics because he relied on his community for clarity and direction.

If you're just starting this emotional journey, you'll need to receive help too. No one knows how to do this on their own. In earlier years, I remember memorizing the wording in books that explained emotions I didn't know how to describe. It was so exciting to make those discoveries. I remember elating, "Oh that's how you say it!"

At the end of this section is a short list of feeling words to get you started with self-awareness. Roll them over in your mind. Look them up in the dictionary. Say them out loud. Notice how it feels in your body. Describe the feeling to a safe friend.

A Clarifying Note on the Word "Safe"

When I refer to the word "safe," I'm talking about emotional safety. When I refer to a "safe friend," I'm talking about someone who is tender and considerate of your feelings and is accepting of you as a person regardless of what their opinion is. They listen and try to understand. They know how important it is for you to feel seen and heard. They don't cut you off to state their position or tell you about something that is more important to them.

You feel emotionally safe with a safe friend.

Drs. Henry Cloud and John Townsend wrote about emotional safety and safe friends in their book *Safe People: How to Find Relationships That Are Good for You and Avoid Those That Aren't.*

It's important to find and interact with emotionally safe people. It's not easy, but they're out there; and are most likely looking for someone themselves to safely connect with. And it is noteworthy to emphasize that you will have to be emotionally vulnerable to others in order to find and determine if someone is emotionally safe for you.

Take it slow. Emotions aren't processed in a rush even within yourself. Start with something positive, then include a moderately negative one. Write down what sticks out to you. Notice an old memory that might pop up when you say it. Process the memory and those feelings with a "safe" listening friend.

A List of Feeling Words:

Love	Worry
Joy	Loneliness
Peace	Emptiness
Anger	Rejection
Fear	Feeling stupid
Sadness	Pride in yourself
Disgust	Satisfaction
Hopeless	On top of the world
Embarrassment	

Sharing with someone to become aware of your feelings is the first step to emotional development. Allowing yourself to continue this sharing with a deeper vulnerability is the gateway to the second stage of emotional development—obtaining validation from others.

2. Share to Feel Validated

Opening ourselves up to express exceptionally embarrassing feelings (like shame or inadequacy) is a terrifying experience because it exposes the most defenseless part of our being. Once we admit these feeling, there is no protective way to take them back.

However, this vulnerability provides the greatest potential for healing because it exposes our deepest emotional pain that needs empathy and validation the most. There is nothing more consoling than to feel seen and heard by someone who understands how painful and difficult a feeling is for us and how courageous we are for talking about it.

Responsibility as a counselor motivated me to locate a support group for a young recovering cocaine addict. He agreed to try it, and I offered to meet him there and participate with him to encourage his attendance. When we first went around the room for introductions I played myself off as a counselor who was there to support a client. But as time passed I felt a nudge to be more authentic and join a group of men dealing with sexual addictive issues. Up to that point I thought my compulsions were something I could work out on my own. (And certainly not something I should admit as a counselor.) But the acceptance and understanding I felt from sharing my struggle in that group of men was so satisfying, I kept coming back long after my client had been taken care of and had eventually moved on to another state.

Sharing vulnerable feelings allows your deepest wounds to receive validation and healing.

There are a growing number of emotional and relational processing groups that are forming. Make sure you look for those that specifically emphasize the processing of emotions, building character, and maturity development; and are not just a general support group or an informational study group. A number of churches offer a program called Celebrate Recovery for people struggling with what they call life's hurts, habits, and hangups. For someone unfamiliar with sharing feelings, this recovery group is a good place to start to experience acceptance and confidentiality.

The groups I am familiar with are:

AliveWell.org/Journey Groups
LifeModelWorks.org/Journey Groups
CreativelyAttached.com
Townsend Leadership Program
Makin Institute for NeuroChange
CelebrateRecovery.org

3. Experience Your Story Anew

Experiencing a validating truth about the shame and inadequacy of a trauma that you had previously experienced alone begins a neural formation in your brain that reshapes and then learns to retell that story from a new and liberating perspective.

In the movie *Good Will Hunting*, Robin Williams's character, a therapist, meets with Matt Damon's character, Will, in a series of strained counseling sessions about the physical abuse Will suffered at the hands of his father. The therapist concludes the sessions by putting his hands on his patient's shoulders, looking into his eyes, and telling him over and over again, "It wasn't your fault! It wasn't your fault!" Experiencing this new validation freed Will to let down his guard to tell his girlfriend he loved her. The movie ended with him jumping in a car to drive across the country to do that!

After experiencing a life-long condition of jaw-clenching anxiety and an avoidance of interactions with people, a family member was finally set free from the fear of being exposed as a bad person. Her liberation came from the validation of someone who accurately described the false shame she had been feeling all these years because as a child she felt like, "No one wanted to be with me."

Experiencing validation increases our courage to risk exploring painful situations that happened to us in our past. We usually learn to understand that whatever did happen wasn't our fault, and the wounds that were inflicted came from individuals who were also hurt in their past.

We learn to forgive and release, and then we begin telling our old story in a new, victorious way. People become excited for us about our new perspective. And that also feels good!

If we have interactive experiences with Jesus, we discover that He had been there all along, saw everything that happened, and hurt right along with us. If we had been a person who was unconsolably angry at Him for not doing anything about it, we might have graphically experienced Him hanging on the cross, saying, "Here's where I was, and here's what I was doing about it!"[12]

All these consolations become a part of our new story that replace the hurts of our old trauma when we felt alone and helpless.

4. Discover Your Authentic Self

Once we experience freedom from the feelings of shame, inferiority, and guilt in our old story, we can let go of our need to control, put up a guard, or push people away to protect ourselves. (See the section heading in chapter 8, "What Gets in the Way: Finding the Link between Past Hurts and Sabotaging Behavior.")

We develop a confident strength to say how we feel, ask for what we want, and act like ourselves. We learn what makes us happy, and we enjoy that about ourselves. Other people notice and like this about us too. It's this emerging true identity that becomes the most attractive and effective part of ourselves. (See chapter 9, "The You You've Always Been.")

A church's relational development group in Fort Wayne, Indiana, describes this authentic transformational process with their motto: "Empowered to discover a new life and recover our true identity." They use validating connections to discover new ways to accept and attune to each other to bring out the best in each of them. One of the teaching leaders in this relational group helped me formulate some of the concepts in this chapter. He uses the same principles effectively in his high school class and applies them at home where his wife comments that she has seen a convincing improvement in his interaction with her and their kids.

Eventually being able to retell my story about what I didn't receive as a boy, and how I substituted sexual fantasies and other compensations to offset that pain, made me realize that I needed to experience healthy, appropriate, enjoyable relationships with women to complete my healing.

Prior to this understanding, admitting I wanted and needed enjoyable feminine interaction would trigger shame in me because these longings had always been tied to sex. When I began to understand that my woman-related needs were legitimate, I began sharing that vulnerably with my wife and other emotionally developed women in my small group. They received my vulnerability with acceptance and affirmation, and I began gaining new confidence and a joy about expressing how I felt, who I was, and what I wanted.

Feeling confident in our authentic self is refreshing and energizing! It's a part of the attractiveness that draws people to us.

As you grow in this confidence, you might also notice these new behaviors in yourself:

- Speaking up with peers who disagree with you.
- Staying relational with your teenagers when they hate you for telling them no.
- Staying collaborative with coworkers who don't like a leadership decision you made.
- Remaining considerate of someone who puts you through a stressful situation. (See chapter 10, "Staying Relational: Even When Life Gets Difficult.")
- Putting your own emotional needs on hold while you attend to the emotional needs of someone else.

Feeling confident in our authentic self is refreshing and energizing! It's a part of the attractiveness that draws people to us.

5. Become Emotionally Available to Others

Once we can act like our true self (without pretense or guardedness) we can make ourselves available emotionally to others. We can relate to what they are going through. Sometimes we do this by admitting a similar weakness. They'll be grateful when we do this because they won't feel alone, and they'll be inclined to open up more about what's going on in their life.

People usually appreciate someone caring about how they feel and wanting to emotionally connect with them. This models a mature way of interacting and influences them to become more emotionally available to others.

As this development grows and you become more emotionally available to others, some of the positive responses you might expect to receive are:

- "You are refreshing to be with!"
- "Your vulnerability encouraged me to be more that way!"
- "I appreciate how you listen so carefully!"
- "Your transparency encouraged me to open up about my own life."

Being emotionally available is one of the most effective ways to positively impact personal and business relationships.

Beginning
It's Okay to Not Know How

4

THERE ARE A NUMBER OF THINGS that many of us don't know how to do. This statement is reasonable to accept but somehow harder to admit when it applies to our personal adeptness—especially for men about dealing with emotions.

However, accepting that we don't know how to do something is a perfect place to start in our emotional development. Feeling inadequate *is* an emotion. Admitting it allows ourselves to feel it and others to connect emotionally with us.

Admitting inadequacy has other benefits. It creates trust with someone because they know we're being honest. It takes the pressure off of them to feel they have to compete with us. And it encourages them to be open (and therefore connectable with others) about their own inadequacies.

So let's make this beginning to emotional development by acknowledging that we don't know how to do it!

It's Okay to Admit

I remember how liberating it felt when I admitted to my recovery group that I didn't know how to change my behavior.
Until then I had tried hard to:

- think the right thoughts
- stop thinking the wrong thoughts
- do what I thought I was supposed to do
- stop doing what everyone else thought I shouldn't do
- make God happy

None of this worked!

When I finally understood I couldn't do it, I realized it was okay to admit it.

The apostle who wrote most of the New Testament epistles made the same confession. He said he couldn't do the things he wanted to do and couldn't stop doing the things he didn't want to do in his own strength (Romans 7:18–19 NLT).

This admission reminds me of a scene from the second season of the TV film series *The Chosen*. Mary Magdalene, full of shame from falling back to her old life, trudged back to camp to reconnect with Jesus. She told Him, "I can't live up to it." He replied, "Well, that's true. But you don't have to. I just want your heart.... The rest will come in time." He not only forgave her, he validated her human inability.

We've all found ourselves like this from time to time—not knowing how to do something.

In similar situations, people in Scripture *didn't know how to do it either*:

- Moses trying to lead over a million people trapped between a revengeful enemy and a drowning sea
- Joseph, in a foreign prison, with no family or legal defense to appeal for him
- Joshua charged with conquering a city fortified with walls wide enough to conduct chariot races
- a bitter, emotionally forsaken Naomi starting over with no evidence of having anything good in her life
- Esther facing the possibility of execution
- Daniel thrown into a den of lions
- three Jewish boys thrown into a fiery furnace

Feeling hopeless and inadequate can cause us to despair. But it's a perfect place to surrender and receive something different. Why not? What would you have to lose?

So let's make this beginning to emotional development by acknowledging that we don't know how to do it.

Upgrades Must Be Downloaded

Even the most advanced computer system can't upgrade itself. It needs a download from a source outside of itself to improve its version.

Our brain's maturation requires the same kind of download to increase its capacity. It grows when it receives downloads from relational interactions with others. We watch people and imitate their higher skills. We "pick up" their healthier attitudes and experience better ways of doing things. We ask people for help and receive not only beneficial advice but the enjoyment of more hands working together to accomplish the task.

Emotional development doesn't happen from our effort. It occurs when we interact relationally with others and download it from them.

Someone Else Has to Perform It

This approach reminds me of a dear friend's heart transplant. Prior to it, his health had failed drastically. He had to quit his job. He felt defeated. He struggled with coping mechanisms to make himself feel better but eventually surrendered those to God and allowed someone's access to the inside of his body to perform heart surgery.

Imagine having your sternum sawn open, your arteries severed, and a plastic machine installed to pump your blood while a new heart is inserted.

My friend had to allow someone else to perform that surgery on him.

A lot of things in life are like that. We become entangled in circumstances that are out of our control. We need help from someone else to get us through it.

That's the willingness my friend agreed to, and the results were marvelous. His health and strength improved. He became energized, positive, and involved in a mission of encouragement that had a far greater impact than he had ever imagined.

It's okay to not know how to do something. Let someone help you.

Healing Happens in Our Inability

My friend George halted me with his words: "Healing happens in our inability." I had to think about that for a moment. I was trying hard to write in a compelling way to convince readers to accept what I was trying to say. When I heard George's comment, I realized that the vulnerable message in this book wouldn't be compelling at all if I wrote it with a smartest, strongest, always-on-top-of-my game persona.

In fact, early on, I realized I didn't have a long track record of success using these relational principles, and I didn't have a set formula guaranteeing readers the results I was writing about. All I had was what I was experiencing—what was working for me and what was giving me hope for the future. A coach and a supportive friend encouraged me to "make the book about your journey instead of a know-it-all how-to book that tells everyone the answers. Write it for your own healing. And then if others are interested, it will be helpful to them. Let God do with it what He wants."

So that's how I wrote from then on—progressing only as fast as I was experiencing it. As if I was teaching myself and gaining clarity from my own writing. The process wasn't pretty. A lot of times it felt painful and frustrating. At one point I quit. Nine months later I reengaged with my writing coach to continue because the relational principles I was experiencing in my life were working. And something inside told me I had to keep going.

Healing does happen in our inability when we involve others in the relational process.

This concept plays itself out in many life stories. For instance:

- Helen Keller's visual inability motivated the development of a worldwide writing system, which came to be known as braille and has helped millions of blind people to read.
- The inability of earlier expeditions to reach the top of the Himalayan mountains motivated the hiring of sherpas to guide and help future climbers.
- My inability to develop a useful website with opt-in functions, scheduling calendars, and auto responders drove me to hire someone with years of experience with exactly what I needed to produce a much better system than anything I had previously attempted.

Many biblical accounts describe successes of people who had no ability to lead people through the life-threatening and humanly impossible situations they were facing. In every case their inability afforded them the opportunity to experience supernatural outcomes that produced far-greater results than anything they could have accomplished on their own:

- The opening of the Red Sea that not only saved millions but lured the entire enemy army into it to be destroyed.
- The crumbling of impenetrable walls established Joshua's credibility as a leader.
- Daniel's inability to save himself produced an impossible reversal that allowed the extermination of the real culprits.
- Three Jewish men surviving an impossible fiery furnace compelled a proud, hardened king to mandate the worship of a God he once derided.

Success can happen in the midst of your inability as well.

Steps to Take

- Accept your limitations and use impossibilities to surrender your tendency to control.
- Move from resisting inability to asking for help.
- Collaborate with people to benefit from their expertise. In return, experience the satisfaction of helping others with yours.
- Give yourself the opportunity to experience enjoyment and success from working together with others.
- Give faith an opportunity to grow by turning over your inability to a power greater than yourself.[13]

The Paradox of Vulnerability
How Strength Comes through Weakness

5

TWO OF MEN'S BIGGEST FEARS are feeling inadequate and looking stupid. Our misinformed masculine culture tells us we have to look like we have it all together. We can't admit failure. And if there is a problem, we have to figure out a way to fix it without asking for help and looking weak.

Unfortunately, this is a damaging message for both men and those closest to them. Being unwilling to talk about our insecurities (or any kind of emotion) not only prevents the possibility of a satisfying and enjoyable connection with someone but also impedes the development of our maturity and true self.

Neuroscience now shows (and I've experienced this first-hand) that our human brain functions at its best and matures the most when it experiences emotional connection with another brain—when we feel seen, felt, and understood by another person.

When this kind of emotional connection happens:

- we calm
- we feel joined and accepted
- we experience relief and joy
- we feel freedom and energy to act like ourself

Vulnerability is the gateway to experiencing this satisfying, enjoyable connection. But it can be misunderstood and misused.

Some Caveats

First, vulnerability isn't about dumping our feelings on someone and expecting them to take care of us. It's about being open and honest to say how we feel and then taking responsibility to ask for what we need.

Learning how to be vulnerable in this responsible way is an example of caring for ourselves and is a prerequisite to knowing how to love others effectively. It's why Jesus made the specific stipulation in Matthew 22:39 to love others the way we love ourselves. This is discussed more thoroughly in chapter 8.

Secondly, we can't be vulnerable with everyone.

Some people are uneasy talking about feelings, so they minimize emotions to make themselves feel comfortable.

Some people are predatory. They use someone's vulnerability to take advantage of them or put the person down.

Worth the Risk

Having shared the above caveats of vulnerability, I want to emphasize its benefits!

If you've never experienced empathy and validation from another person with whom you've been vulnerable, the thought of trying it is probably terrifying. However it's a beneficial risk worth taking, and I want you to experience the opportunity!

So in the remaining chapter I offer encouraging examples of how vulnerability can result in positive outcomes—five ways sharing a perceived weakness can result in our greatest strength.

1. Creates Trust

My oldest son is a high school teacher who stands in front of hundreds of students each week attempting to capture their attention and get them to learn what he tries to teach. It's natural for him to be open and honest about his weaknesses, and he notices that whenever he acts like himself, his students respond more openly and favorably to him.

Henry Cloud wrote, "Trust is built through showing appropriate vulnerability. We trust people who will show us their imperfections and do not lord over us with some sort of façade of 'having it all together.' People who share where they have had to overcome obstacles or are struggling with hard things are more easily trusted than the ones who look like they never had to struggle. We cannot trust people who are too 'perfect.'"[14]

My son says a common ground of trust and respect develops between himself and his students when he vulnerably takes responsibility for his shortcomings.

2. Deepens a Connection

I was a member of a small group of men who met once a month to do emotional processing. I'll never forget one particular meeting when our leader emphasized the need to share feelings so each of us could more effectively experience what the other person was going through.

An older guy began the session sharing with tears about an end-of-life experience he was afraid of going through with a loved one. He talked about the pain he was anticipating and his wish to avoid experiencing it. The look and the wetness in the other men's eyes made it undeniably clear that they understood. He appreciated them being "in it" with him. Their affirmation made him feel normal and gave him a realistic perspective and a spark of hope that he would be able to get through it.

A young man shared a success. It was a huge encouragement for him compared to the many painful defeats he had experienced in childhood. The group enjoyed celebrating his accomplishment and helped him realize the importance of cherishing and holding on to the memory of this victorious experience.

A successful businessman shared his hidden insecurities and his realization that action was necessary on his part to come out of his painful, isolated depression—to say how he felt, take responsibility for what he wanted, and ask people for help. The group validated his pain and affirmed that the effort he was exerting was worth continuing.

Another guy shared a regrettable decision he had been agonizing over for a long time that he said had cost him the most important thing in his life. The emphasis on sharing feelings in the group helped him risk exposing his devastation. The acceptance he received generated hope that different decisions were possible in the future that could bring him success.

Before the meeting these men carried unprocessed pain and unfulfilled celebration, keeping it alone inside of themselves. Once feelings were shared, they were available to be felt by others, which helped lighten the painful ones and increase the joyful ones.

Healing deepens and enjoyable potential increases when we vulnerably share both our painful failures and our proud moments with one another.

A good friend related how an inner, empty part of himself had felt unnoticed, uncared about, and alone since childhood. He realized the need to connect more with someone to resolve this, so we arranged weekly call times to connect. He said just the anticipation of having someone reach out to him who was interested in listening made him feel better.

3. Helps Us Step into Our True Self

Lonnie met me at the café one morning to review a new section of my book. He was a good friend, and I valued his input.

His response to what I shared began with encouraging comments and then segued into a lot of creative suggestions with quotes from other authors I hadn't thought of.

That's when I started to shut down. I couldn't process everything he was saying fast enough, and it felt like I had incompetently left out a lot of good material.

I hadn't yet developed the emotional capacity to override my inferiority, so feelings of condemnation started to overtake me. I began accusing myself: "You can't write this book! You're not capable! Lonnie understands all this stuff better than you do. Get out of here! Run away to escape this uncomfortable feeling."

My facial expression must have communicated it because he said, "You're starting to look overwhelmed!"

I had closed my eyes, lowered my head, and propped it up with my arms resting on the café table. I didn't have the strength to look up at him or even form words to describe how I felt.

Lonnie patiently sat there and waited. Then he gently nudged me with the reminder that there was a difference between the shameful, inferior little boy part of me and my true adult self. He gave me time and space to begin processing this. Comfort and confidence began to grow as I felt the presence of an accepting person who was glad to be with me regardless of how immature I was reacting.

As I vulnerably allowed myself to receive his acceptance, I was able to separate the inferior part of me from my true self and something began to shift:

- I calmed.
- I felt my true self come back "on-line."
- I was thankful I didn't run away.
- I was proud of letting myself go through this hard experience so my capacity could grow.

The shameful, inadequate feelings began subsiding. In a few minutes I felt free and alive again.

Allowing myself to feel inferior and then accepted in someone's presence regulated my emotions that were shutting down. Through this process, new neural pathways grew in the emotional side of my brain. These new pathways became the increased emotional capacity that I would be able to access the next time this reaction occurred.

4. Makes Us More Effective

I've often experienced a self-conscious inferiority when I felt the focus of a conversation shift to me. It could happen when I talked with an unfamiliar person, and especially when I spoke in front of an audience.

Insecurity would surge up inside of me and start yelling, "You're not adequate! What you're saying isn't impactful!"

The more I felt it "yell," the harder I'd try to say it differently to impress my listeners. The distraction would become immobilizing. Faces in the audience would blur as the tension overtook my thinking. Even when I tried to care about someone by asking their name, I would forget it in an instant because I wasn't listening in the first place.

Until I learned this secret: I shared how I felt!

I'd be appropriate about how much I shared, but I'd be honest. I'd say, "I'm feeling insecure for some reason." Or I'd pose a question: "Do you ever feel inferior speaking in front of people and find yourself trying too hard to make a good impression?" And then I'd admit: "It's like that for me right now. It feels forced, and I'm not acting like myself."

Just acknowledging this feeling to myself would feel grounding, and especially when I noticed affirmation from the person or audience I was addressing—a head nod, a smile, or a look of admiration in their eyes. At this point I would feel myself relax. The tension in my head would release. The pressure to perform would lessen, and words began flowing more naturally. I would feel more like my true self and my communication became more effective.

5. Builds Favor with Others

That's what I mean about becoming more attractive! It's not about looks. It's about becoming more favorable to people.

In my younger intern years as a counselor, I naively allowed one of my adolescent clients to access Myspace (an early social media platform) during a session with her. The court-ordered kids in the group home where I worked were hard to reach, so I was willing to do anything to gain their trust and establish a rapport with them. I felt pretty "cool" for letting her do this until she told me she contacted the out-of-state predator who got her into trouble to begin with.

I was aghast! The blood drained from my head as soon as I realized what had happened, and the counseling session came to an abrupt halt!

As she left my office, I knew that within hours everyone on campus—the other kids, her house parents, and my boss—would hear about it. I felt helplessly exposed and totally ashamed of my poor judgement. Even though I was a licensed therapist, a grandparent, and an ordained minister, my immediate survival response was to either:

- lie and deny it, or
- get in my car, drive away, and never come back!

Thankfully I remembered that honesty was the best policy, and trusting in God's grace would probably result in a better outcome. So that's what I did the next morning when I received a knock at my door from the program director and my supervisor who asked, "May we come in and talk?"

With my pulse pumping faster than normal and my face feeling flushed, I was honest about everything that happened. My admission turned out well. They recognized my heart and realized my good intention. My supervisor ended the conversation by saying, "We like how you think outside the box. Just don't do that again!"

That vulnerability helped build credibility with my superiors. Later in my employment they showed me great favor by funding an out-of-state training that launched me into the emotional and relational approach I use in ministry to this day and am writing about in this book!

The risk of looking weak by admitting my failure resulted in a great strength!

An Encouragement

Learning to be vulnerable is a process. You don't have to be perfect at it. And as we've discussed earlier, you don't have to know how to do it to begin. It starts off slowly and develops over time and with practice. Review chapter 3, "Understanding the Journey: The 5 Stages of Emotional Development."

Try It with Someone

Sharing our personal stuff isn't easy. In fact, it's terrifying if you haven't done it before because once you do, you know it's out there, and you can't take it back.

The truth is, there are thousands of people who struggle with the same issues you do. But you won't know that unless you interact with them in a real and vulnerable way.

When you do, it will be satisfying.

Try it with someone you trust—someone who will listen. I think you will appreciate it!

Grasping a New Paradigm
Knowing the Kindness of God Helps You Let Down Your Guard

6

ELVIS PRESLEY was all the musical rage in 1956. He was making his first appearance on the *Ed Sullivan TV Show* that fall, and I wanted to see him perform! As a young boy I'd listen for hours to singles on my 45 RPM record player; I would mimic lyrics and imagine myself performing them. As early as first grade, I asked my teacher for permission to stand in front of the class to sing "Davy Crockett: King of the Wild Frontier."

That night I really wanted to see Elvis, but my mother said, "No! You have to go to bed."

I was devastated—bewildered, at first, because the show aired early in the evening. It was still daylight and there was no urgency to go to bed. It was the disregard in my mother's tone that made matters worse. My disappointment quickly turned to anger—rage actually! It probably wasn't the first time I had experienced this disregard, but this evening's experience was the straw that broke the camel's back. Something inside me snapped and then erupted into a defiant vow: "If nobody cares how I feel, I'll make *myself* famous to get the attention I want; and do whatever it takes to make me happy!"

Detrimental to My Real Needs

The vow embedded a paradigm of thinking that would damage my life for decades. I began living it out with achievements during high school—student officer positions, recognition as a *Chicago Tribune* football All-Star, and a Mr. Americanism Award. It continued into adulthood with an unconscious drive to control and achieve whatever I thought would make me feel significant.

It's tragic to think how deceived I was about what I thought would make me happy. This self-determination blocked all opportunity to receive what my soul needed the most: love, regard, and a sense of belonging in relationships with people.

Detrimental to My Christian Life

Even after a spiritual conversion at the age of twenty-two, this underlying drive to perform undermined my full devotion to Christ as I wanted to obtain a leadership position in my church. The importance of compassionate relationships that would normally accompany a complete devotion to Christ was lacking in my pursuit of attention. I focused my energy on keeping the rules and doing everything possible that would get me approval.

My spiritual conversion did expose me to a heart-warming reception from the church people I had left behind after graduating from high school. But as wonderful as this new love was, the deep-seated but unresolved emotional vow I made as a child led me to fall back into a performance-based mindset. This vow and my fear of disapproval shaped my perception of God as an exacting judge intent on weeding unacceptable people out of His kingdom.

At that younger and less emotionally developed point in life, I thought performance was the most important thing to Him!

I remember standing outside of church psyching myself up to go in and act more loving, patient, and calm. That determination lasted only a few short moments until my people-pleasing insecurities got triggered again and I reverted back to performance to get approval.

At bedtime I remember reciting a list of prayers, without ever considering to talk with God honestly about what was important to me.

I thought performance
was the most important thing to Him.

Detrimental to My Health and Others

High school classmates noticed my obsessive drive. One friend saw me straining to play impressive guitar leads in our band and said, "Doug, you're trying too hard!"

A Sunday School classmate said, "The only time you show up for church is after you get a good newspaper write-up about a football game you played in the Friday night before."

Chapter 2 recounts how emotional connections with my family suffered because of my unconscious drive for significance. This drive culminated in an emotional breakdown in my late forties.

A Shift in Focus

Hitting rock bottom forced me to change. But it took a long time to recover fully, especially in terms of accepting a completely new paradigm of thinking.

My mentor told me: "The only thing that will heal you is involvement in relationships." My attachment pain came from a relationship, so the healing of it would have to come from relationships.

This reliance on relationships was unfamiliar and hard to grasp, and it felt scary. I had no previous experience doing it. But my overwhelming anger and rage forced me to surrender my isolated attempts to fix it. That's when I called for help.

I experienced the empathy, acceptance, and affirmation I needed for my childhood attachment pain in those early mentoring sessions. I discovered that letting down my guard to experience this emotional connection was a lot easier and more consoling than forcing myself to act like I had it all together.

This new relational approach became a source of comfort, so I sought out more of it. I asked others for what I needed. I began to see the value of collaborating with people more than trying to fix everything by myself.

How It Changed My Paradigm of God

I began applying my relational experiences with people to interactions with God, and soon I experienced the same kind of acceptance from Him. I realized He hadn't been trying to weed me out. He had been trying to draw me in.

God's Kindness Helps Us Embrace Vulnerability

When we realize it is the kindness of God that helps us make difficult but beneficial changes in our lives (Romans 2:4 ESV), we become more willing to be honest with Him about what we're feeling.

The following verses from Scripture encourage this kind of vulnerability:

- Correction is normal and should be expected. It's "the way of life" (Proverbs 6:23 NKJV).
- God knows "we are dust" (Psalm 103:14 NKJV) and are "limited" in our human thoughts (Psalm 94:11 TLB).
- We're not expected to know the right way to go by ourselves (Jeremiah 10:23).
- Jesus's intention is to restore us. He said He didn't come to condemn (John 3:17).
- God's desire is for all of us to be saved (2 Peter 3:9).
- He makes enjoyable provision amidst attacks from our adversaries (Psalm 23:5).
- His goodness and mercy follow us all the days of our lives (Psalm 23:6).

Realizing God's kindness helps us let down our protective guard to trust Him more.

God Wants to Be with Us in Our Mess

Jesus's birth in a stable illustrates God's desire to be with us in the most nasty and undesirable conditions of our lives. In the film *The Chosen Christmas Special* (2021), Joseph had to scoop cow dung off the filthy barn floor to clear enough space for his wife to lie down and give birth to the Son of God. The owner of the inn had no rooms available but offered clean linens to wrap the newborn in, some of which were used to line the unsanitary horse trough where they laid Him.

Jesus's birth in that barn filth demonstrates His willingness to enter into ours. It's a picture of how necessary His presence is to heal our dirtiest circumstance and subsequent pain.

Grasping the New Paradigm

You know how it feels when you are standing in line and someone pushes against you? You brace yourself and push back! The same reaction takes place when someone attacks you in an argument.

But have you experienced how it feels when an opposing person acknowledges a legitimate point you were trying to make? How your defenses lessen and you become more considerate of their position?

That's how vulnerable admission catalyzes transformation. Admitting failure, or inability, and setting aside our defenses often softens the heart of the other person to be able to consider something they hadn't thought of.

In the same way, letting down our guard creates space for us to change and transform into our true identity. We become free to experiment with our inclinations to find what gives us enjoyment, what we are effective at, and what others appreciate about us.

Understanding the kindness of God gives us the courage to let down our guard and be able to experience this transformation.

It's Not Good to Be Alone
(Even When God Is with You)

7

NO MATTER HOW VIVID COLORS of scarlet and purple paint a sunset sky, or how still and delicate a fog hangs over an early morning Smokey Mountain valley, those breathtaking scenes can feel empty if we don't have someone to share them with.

I recall a college boat excursion on the Atlantic Ocean where I enjoyed watching the evening moonlight sparkle on the ship's wake. But a longing gnawed at me, especially when I saw a couple standing close together at the bow of the ship. I longingly wondered if someone in a faraway state was looking up at the same stars and thinking about me.

Or there was the time I felt disappointment after a Sunday church service because I thought my wife-to-be was out of town. Something inside of me felt empty until a leap in my heart noticed her standing in the crowd of women gathered on the other side of the lunchroom.

It seems life and beauty are meant to be shared with someone. Enjoyment gets amplified when it's experienced with another person. Love songs are felt more deeply when the person we are singing about is sitting in the audience.

And even in difficult situations, a shared connection with another person can calm our painful emotion without changing any of the precipitating circumstances.

I remember an enjoyable jam-packed two weeks of great food and many laughs with my sister and her family on a Florida visit. We played games, went on a scenic bike ride, and attended a PGA golf tournament. But returning home brought back to mind all my caretaking responsibilities. Focusing on that pulled me back into depression until I remembered the friends I could call who would understand how I felt. Ensuing phone conversations with two listening buddies lifted my spirits.

Our brains were created to function at their best when they experience enjoyable connections with other brains.

That's why God told Adam it wasn't good for him to be alone even as He was standing right next to him in the garden. (Genesis 2:18). God's ability to provide didn't feel threatened when He told Adam this because God exists in a Triune relationship, so He understood how Adam would need the same kind of enjoyable connection with another human.

The Necessary Horizontal Component

Jesus said, "The entire law and all the demands of the prophets" (Matthew 22:40 NLT) are based on two commandments:

- Love God
- Love Others

He said the loving God part is "the first and greatest commandment" (verse 38 NLT). Doing this with all our heart, soul, and mind is the vertical and most obvious component of devotion to God. But Jesus also said, "A second is equally important: 'Love your neighbor as yourself'" (verse 39 NLT). This is the horizontal and often less recognized component of devotion.

But Paul, the great Apostle to the New Testament church, explained how important love toward others is as an expression of true faith. He said, "The whole law [of God] can be summed up in this one command: 'Love your neighbor as yourself'" (Galatians 5:14, see also verse 6, NLT). The Jewish law he was referring to is found in Leviticus 19, which contains no less than fifteen commands pertaining to how we should relate with one another.

Our independent world and its human inclination to trust in our own "understanding" (Proverbs 3:5 NLT) makes working in isolation more comfortable to us. And with increasing stressors in life, it just feels a lot easier to stay home and relax.

But in these later years I've experienced the benefits of making emotional connection with people, myself, and God. Now I take more initiative to do that because it produces a life-giving energy and a satisfaction that offsets empty feelings from attachment pain.

How It Benefits Us

The horizontal component of connecting with and loving our neighbor is not only a command; it benefits all of us who do it. Our emotional and physical workload lightens. If we fall, someone is there to pick us up. Two people working together get exponentially more done than two people working separately. And our energy is more sustainable when we collaborate together.

For years when I read the Bible chapter in Philippians about God being the "supplier of *all* our needs," I assumed His provision would come directly and only from Him. So, I thought, He would be all I needed. After experiencing encouragement and consolation from interactions with friends during these past difficult years, I've realized how much of God's provision comes through other people. This obvious truth now stands out as I read the same chapter with Paul referencing specific people and others who helped him: "Clement…and the rest of my fellow workers," "my true teammate [Epaphroditus]," and the "women [who] worked side by side with me" (Philippians 4:3, see verse 18, TLB).

And the writer to the Hebrews explains another benefit—how daily connecting spiritually with each other keeps our heart from becoming hardened against God (Hebrews 3:13 TLB).

The horizontal component of connecting with and loving our neighbor is not only a command; it benefits all of us who do it.

What Is Connection?

In her book *Atlas of the Heart*, Brené Brown wrote, "Across my research, I define connection as the energy that exists between two people when they feel seen, heard, and valued; when they can give and receive without judgment; and when they derive sustenance and strength from the relationship."[15] I would add to that definition the feeling of being delighted in and wanted. I especially relate to Brené Brown's use of the word *energy* in her description. I often feel more motivation after a good connecting conversation with a friend.

This connection happened recently, when two people in my small group texted, "We're planning to head to the coffee shop. Anyone want to join us?" I had gotten up late, felt groggy that morning, and didn't want to go. I argued with myself about staying home but then thought I better do what I'm writing about in this book. So I joined them at the coffee shop, and we connected! It turned out well. We enjoyed a pleasant conversation about past adventures and our love of plants. Nothing dramatic was shared, and we didn't solve any problems. But I felt more energized, awake, and much better after we talked.

The Consequences of Disconnection

In the same book Brené Brown cites "a meta-analysis of studies on loneliness" where researchers found that even though conditions of air pollution, obesity, and excessive drinking shorten our odds of living a long life, living with loneliness "increases our odds of dying early by 45%."[16] She cites a 2017 *Harvard Business Review* article by Dr. Vivek Murthy, who writes, "During my years caring for patients, the most common pathology I saw was not heart disease or diabetes; it was loneliness."[17]

Brené Brown also quotes John Cacioppo's neuroscientific work on loneliness: "Loneliness is not just a sad condition—it's a dangerous one." He explains, "When we feel isolated, disconnected, and lonely, we try to protect ourselves. In that mode, we want to connect, but our brain is attempting to override connection with self-protection. That means less empathy, more defensiveness, more numbing, and less sleeping. Unchecked loneliness fuels continued loneliness by keeping us afraid to reach out." Disconnection weakens our stamina and potential. "We don't derive strength from our rugged individualism," says Cacioppo, "but rather from our collective ability to plan, communicate, and work together."[18]

In chapter 9 of her book, Brown explains how a lack of authentic connection with people makes us want to change our behavior to fit in. Trying to fit in prevents the development of our true identity.

As I discuss in chapter 9, "The You You've Always Been," allowing our true identity to develop uncovers "the most attractive and effective part of yourself." Acting the way we think others want us to act prevents the discovery of this satisfying and effective part of ourselves.

Having covered what connection is and what devastating consequences result from not having it, I want to explore some benefits of connection in what follows.

A Catalyst to Physical Healing

Healthy emotional connections correlate with healthy bodies.

In the mid-1990s the Centers for Disease Control did a large medical study with Kaiser Permanente. The study involved 17,500 adults and revealed a huge correlation between Adverse Childhood Experiences (ACE Trauma) and an "increased risk of seven out of the top 10 causes of death." The researchers found that even though someone "didn't smoke, didn't drink, had normal cholesterol, were not overweight, and exercised regularly," they still "had a 360% increased risk of heart disease if they had experienced seven out of 10 ACE trauma indicators."[19] This study shows the correlation between disease and unhealthy, traumatic relationships.

Conversely, effects of these diseases could be greatly reduced. A big part of that healing can come from experiencing someone connect emotionally with you about the trauma you suffered—so that you feel seen, heard, and joined in the pain of that adversity.

Opens Awareness to Him

Even though the Bible says, "My sheep hear My voice" (John 10:27 NKJV), some of us have difficulty feeling God's presence and hearing what He says. It's true of me when I am alone and especially when I feel emotional pain. However being with other people and sensing their interest and camaraderie in whatever I'm going through opens my awareness more to what an invisible God is trying to convey.

Jesus validated the success of this interactive approach by saying, "Where two or three people gather in my name, I am there with them" (Matthew 18:20 NIRV).

Carolyn Carney, the national director of spiritual formation for InterVarsity Christian Fellowship/USA, emphasized "how [relationally] attached we are to God" determines our most effectiveness in prayer with Him. In her book *The Power of Group Prayer* she explains how this attachment principal correlates with the relational factors that make groups more effective in prayer because they have to "use collective wisdom to discern," "listen" to, and synchronize with each other in order to successfully connect with Him.[20]

Connecting relationally with people opens our receptivity to God.

I recall a young, newly married man who told me how his ability to recognize God's love increased when he experienced the unconditional love of his wife.

I've found this to be true as well. A group of therapists and lay ministers called a meeting to discuss forming a supportive network for each other, and they invited me. I felt honored to be included but expressed a limited capacity to be able to invest in the organization they wanted to establish. It didn't matter to them. They said they were glad I was there. Just feeling them want me energized my hope that God was answering my prayers and giving direction to my life.

Something Greater Than Our Pain

The satisfying effect of sharing our emotional turmoil with someone and then feeling them connect with us functions like a teeter-totter—offsetting our emotional pain on one end with something more satisfying and relieving on the other. When we experience an accepting, attuning connection with someone, the painful circumstance we're in may not go away, but it gets outweighed—on the other end—with an experience that is more enjoyable.

I remember the moment my little granddaughter jumped onto my lap and nuzzled her head into my chest, expecting me to wrap my arms around and squeeze the daylights out of her. I did! And I enjoyed every second of it. It offset every negative emotion I was feeling at the time.

I remember the time my oldest grandson—a junior at a Big Ten University—escorted *his grandpa* around campus letting me affectionately slip my hand inside his arm as we walked among his peers across the campus lawn. Without experiencing any embarrassment in him, I felt cherished and greatly valued.

Or the memory of my boyhood dog looking up into my eyes, pawing at my arm, and enjoying me pet the top of his silky head. I can still feel his appreciation, smell his fur and bad breath as he panted away at me with gratitude. I knew he loved me, and I loved him. We both felt connected and belonged to each other. Just thinking about that memory today produces an appreciation that offsets some emptiness or negativity I may be experiencing at the time.

I witnessed a bumblebee in our back yard flitting determinedly from one flower to another to find more nectar. It wasn't deterred when I tried to spray it away with my garden hose. In the same determined way the relational circuitry in our brain is relentlessly trying to connect with the circuitry in other brains to find the sweet satisfaction of connection with someone else to help offset loneliness and emotional pain.

In one last example from my own life: I received an unexpected expression of love from the guys in our monthly emotional process group as I shared a painful experience. One of them blurted out, "I just want to say how much I love you for letting yourself be so open and vulnerable about how you feel. I can so relate to it." I teared up, and then he and a bunch of them gathered around to hug me. This good memory lingered for days. Upon waking one morning with a depressive thought, I remembered this experience again and correlated it to how God says He loves me. This experience produced an appreciation that lasted for the remainder of the day. And still did for days after that.

Avoiding Self-Destructive Behavior

In his TED Talk, *Everything You Think You Know about Addiction Is Wrong*,"[21] Johann Hari cited an early twentieth-century experiment that challenged typical thinking about addiction. Individual rats were isolated in a cage and given the option to drink plain water or water laced with heroin and cocaine. In this isolated environment, Hari said, "the rat will almost always prefer the drug water and almost always kill itself quite quickly."

Later in the seventies Professor Bruce Alexander from Vancouver expanded on that experiment. He offered the same drug choice to a group of rats in a "Rat Park," where he said they were provided with "loads of cheese, loads of colored balls, loads of tunnels, loads of friends." In that environment, he said, the rats "don't like the drug water. They almost never use it. None of them overdose. You go from almost 100 percent overdose when they're isolated to zero percent overdose when they have happy connected lives."

Alexander also researched the results of soldiers returning from Vietnam where 20 percent of them had been using "loads of heroin" while in service there. He said, "The Archives of General Psychiatry did a really detailed study" and found that "95 percent of them just stopped" when they got reintegrated into society. Professor Alexander began to wonder, "What if addiction is an adaptation to your [isolated] environment?"

Hari also cited Professor Peter Cohen of the Netherlands as saying, "Maybe we shouldn't even call it addiction. Maybe we should call it bonding. Human beings have a natural and innate need to bond, and when we're happy and healthy, we'll bond and connect with each other, but if you can't do that, because you're traumatized or isolated or beaten down by life, you will bond with something that will give you some sense of relief." He listed some of these relieving sources as gambling, pornography, cocaine, and cannabis. He said, "You will bond and connect with something because that's our nature."

"Disconnection is a major driver of addiction," Hari concluded.

I can attest to this. I'm much more prone to give in to addictive habits when I'm alone. On one occasion I was surprised by the unusual contentment I felt attending a public art exhibit where old compensations of sexual and romantic fantasies from childhood attachment pain usually would have been triggered. On this occasion I was amazed that none of those feelings were present, and then I remembered

I had just come from a very satisfying coffee shop conversation with another person. I was emotionally "filled up" from that enjoyable experience and had no need to utilize any of those "sources" Professor Cohen referred to that "we bond with to give some sense of relief."

Johann Hari concluded his Ted Talk with the insightful statement: "The opposite of addiction is not sobriety. The opposite of addiction is connection."

"Disconnection is a major driver of addiction."

That's why God told Adam it wasn't good for him to be alone.

Set Your Intention

I know when we feel emotional pain it's easier and seems safer to stay isolated. It still feels like that to me some days. But I've learned that healing can only take place in healthy, love-bonded relationships. So I call someone or get together with a community that loves and values me. As stated before, it was a relationship (or lack thereof) that hurt us. It will take a relationship to heal us.

Relational connection is the catalyst to emotional healing, offsetting pain, recognizing God's presence, and avoiding self-destructive behavior.

Would you consider coming out of your self-protecting isolation to experience these benefits?

The Necessity of Receiving
Instead of Striving to Obtain What You Want

8

ALEX CALLED TO SCHEDULE an appointment with a potential recovery sponsor for his opioid dependence. But that wasn't all he was dealing with. He was feeling guilty because he had loaned his motorcycle to a family member who was then killed in an accident. He had also lost money in some failed investments. His critical father was a successful investor, and Alex felt ashamed to admit to him that he failed in this endeavor.

When Alex showed up for the appointment, he ramped up his efforts to impress the potential sponsor with all that he knew and everything he had accomplished. Unfortunately, that striving to impress didn't do anything to comfort his painful guilt and the shame. He was trying to suppress painful emotions and was striving hard to achieve some kind of feel-good experience about himself.

But neither of those solutions works. What Alex needed most was compassion from someone who understood how he felt and was willing to join him in his pain so he wouldn't feel so alone and agitated with doubt and emotional turmoil. The only way he could experience this was by being vulnerable about his feelings and letting himself receive consolation from someone else.

The purpose of this book is to help you understand that this is what people need, and this is what you need to be able to give. And this chapter is about how to do that!

The answer is in learning how to receive, and then learning how to make yourself emotionally available so others can receive from you.

If we have friends and communities who are willing to be vulnerable and interact with each other like this, we'll find that asking for and receiving what we need is a lot easier and more effective than striving so hard to achieve success on our own.

An interesting note about writing this chapter is that I struggled to adequately convey the emotional content of it in the beginning. I had to call a good friend to process that feeling and experience an insight to be able to get started.

As we've already discussed: feeling seen, known, understood, and enjoyed by another person is the emotional experience that makes our brain operate at its best. All we have to do is cooperate with it.

The challenges are:

- being open to allow that,
- being willing to share how we feel,
- being vulnerable to let someone into our private world,
- being willing to listen,
- being willing to slow down and consider another perspective,
- being open to receive.

Learning to receive will make you more effective in four major areas of life:

- accomplishments
- emotional health
- relationships
- spirituality

Let me explain.

Accomplishments

Receiving help from others increases the likelihood of accomplishing our aspirations. My friend Lonnie, who is experienced in the Townsend Leadership Training program, often refers to Dr. Townsend's saying that the people who are most successful in life are those who are the most highly resourced—in other words, the ones who receive the most help from other people.

It's ironic. The professional athletes whom we criticize for making insane amounts of money do so by obtaining a huge amount of support, advice, and training from other people: coaches, physical trainers, offensive and defensive coordinators, advisors, nutritionists, doctors, analysts, and psychological mentors. In this respect they are smarter than many of us "criticizers" who attempt to do life and mission alone. These athletes are willing to receive whatever help is available to make themselves better. And the Olympic medal winners who stand on the platform (even those who qualify to participate in the Olympics) have only accomplished this by receiving help and training of others, support of sponsors, and encouragement of friends, mentors, and family members.

Receiving help is the secret to success and to the accomplishment of our highest goals.

Looking back, I see that the real successes in my life have only come from receiving resources outside of myself: opportunities that were presented, leads that were given, the Spirit of God, and people who directed and gave me advice.

These include:

- a revelation that Jesus is the Son of God
- a divinely presented love that softened my heart

81

- a community that offered acceptance and belonging
- a supportive wife
- influential people who directed me
- monetary provision in desperate times
- a calling that changed my life
- a lucrative international sales opportunity
- a unique house that was affordable
- an invitation to play in a band
- connection with a coach who helped me write this book

In every case, these were resources presented to me. Receiving and acting on them was my part, but I didn't create them. Even personal changes needed throughout my life were initiated from ideas, suggestions, and resources I received outside of myself.

Relational interactions with people help us become aware of what we need and provide the resources to meet those needs. Refusal to collaborate with others is the limiting factor of many great ideas and endeavors. (More later in the chapter about how we unconsciously sabotage the reception of beneficial resources.)

Developing Emotional Health

"Receiving always precedes giving" is a principal that applies to the development of healthy emotional maturity. It's a quote from the book *Living from the Heart Jesus Gave You*.[22] This statement refers to the unconditional love an infant needs to receive in order to develop in an emotionally healthy way. Without experiencing this, a deficit exists in the child's attachment system that cries out for it and prevents further emotional development—sometimes for a lifetime—until this need is met.

The emotional need to receive is not only limited to infancy. It's what helps us experience positive corrective experiences about any difficult situation even as we get older.

Let me share an illustration from my own adult life.

Even before the hour-and-twenty-minute drive home from band practice ended, I started to feel an encouraging shift from the hopeless despair I expressed earlier to the group.

We were supposed to have practiced for an upcoming gig, but when my band members heard my emotional pain, their focus changed. One member earnestly committed to praying hope for me. The other listened with "eyes" that told me he understood, appreciated what I shared, and cared deeply about it.

The consolation of having received this love is what I felt as I pulled into my back-alley garage. It made me more appreciative of a warm welcome when I walked into the house. The rest of the day was peaceful, and by evening my healthier state of mind was open to a new hope-giving idea that popped into my head as I gratefully rehearsed the events of the day with my wife.

Being open and willing to receive creates opportunities that increase our joy and emotional health.

Satisfying Relationships

Being able to receive love shows us how to effectively give love to others—which increases the likelihood of developing an enjoyable relationship with them. That's why Jesus made the specific stipulation (noted in the preceding chapter) to love others the way we love ourselves.

Which begs the questions:

Do you love yourself?
Are you *willing* to?
Do you know how?
Are you willing to receive it?

Loving yourself includes:

- being honest with yourself
- caring about your feelings instead of avoiding them
- sharing your feelings with others and asking for their help to get your needs met

Refusal to receive limits the establishment of satisfying relationships, and it often contributes to the deterioration of relationships we already have.

Denise was a smart young grad student who had a sincere belief in God and a desire to help others. But she would insist on doing so without first considering how the recipient would feel about it. She hadn't received this kind of consideration as a little girl, so she didn't know how to give it as an adult. People would feel uncomfortable and pressured with her attempts to help them, which made it difficult and sometimes unsafe for them to say no. Unaddressed childhood pain made her uncomfortable in healthy, loving environments, so she avoided them. As a result, her emotional needs didn't get met and she would insist on helping others as a means to fill that void which pushed them away.

In my emotionally underdeveloped years I did the same thing as a church leader. A young man related his disappointment of not having heard from me in a long time. He said, "I thought I had a friend who was interested in me." Without him naming anyone, I knew he was talking about me. And rightly so. I had reached out to him, initially, because I thought he needed a father figure. It seemed like a good ministry idea, and I thought God would be pleased if I did it. But looking back, my gesture was more about what gave me satisfaction than what he needed in the long term. Not having addressed my unmet attachment needs kept me unconsciously preoccupied with trying to get those needs met, which prevented the development of my emotional capacity to give the young man the ongoing consideration and consistency he needed.

Receiving acceptance, enjoyable connection, and help from people is a prerequisite to becoming an effective lover of others.

That's why Jesus made the specific stipulation to love others the way we love ourselves.

A Connection with God

Being able to receive is also a prerequisite to experiencing a connection with God. John 1:12 makes this implication by stating, "But as many as received Him, to them He gave the right to become children of God…" (NKJV). God wants to connect with us. We have to be willing to receive to let Him.

The fact that God "first loved us" (1 John 4:19 NKJV) and "chose us" (Ephesians 1:4 NKJV)—we didn't first choose Him—are often unrealized attributes of God. Reception is the only way we can respond to these beneficial attributes. We can't create them, and we can't enhance them with our own effort.

It took my grandpa a long time to experience the fulfillment in life he had been looking for by utilizing this principle of receiving. His striving to find the "grass that looked greener on the other side of the fence" moved him from one farm to another when he was a younger man—grandma said they relocated "thirty-one times in thirty years." His frustration increased when the church he attended removed his membership because he filed bankruptcy. He thought he had been living "just as good as all the other members."

But one morning he burst into our farmhouse kitchen yelling, "I found it!"

I thought he was talking about his minnow bucket. He had complained about losing it on a previous fishing trip, but in this instance he was referring to something much more significant. He had experienced a dream about angels scrubbing out his heart because they said, "The Lord wants to move in." From that experience he awoke with a new outlook on life. His recollection wasn't theologically accurate, but it illustrated the point that something far greater than his own striving had to be received in order for him to experience this new outlook.

He received additional revelations over the coming days and weeks:

- a presence that came down from above to shield him from condemning accusations
- an image of nail holes in a hand to show that a price had been paid for his sins

These fulfilling, life-changing experiences were all something he received apart from his own unsuccessful striving.

And that is why he was yelling when he burst into our farmhouse kitchen.

My experience was similar!

I worked hard in younger years to get attention. Most of my effort was consumed with athletics and playing in a rock 'n roll band until my birthdate placed me #4 in the Vietnam draft.

Having written an appeal to the US Army requesting alternative service, I found myself sitting in the living room of my former church youth leader. I had included him in the religious story I concocted, and the army required a signed affidavit from people I wrote about who had influenced me.

The youth leader challenged my self-righteous beliefs with an impactful question that jolted me with a supernatural revelation that Jesus *is* the Son of God. When I met with him again a week later, his prayer brought me to tears as I experienced an overwhelming sense that God loved me.

The reception of these experiences changed my life. And more followed:

- Welcoming arms from church members I hadn't seen for years.
- A dear white-haired lady asserting herself across the room to say: "Douglas, you don't know how glad we are to see you!"
- The minister who cried and the Spirit who entered my heart when I said, "I want to repent."
- Subsequent revelations that included: a wife, career steps, provisions, forgiveness, and open doors to the future.

Years later, and whenever I'd slip off track again—striving to pursue my own ways—this principle of receiving would reappear to get me back on course. When I'd be at my wit's end in a seemingly unsolvable circumstance, the promise from Nehemiah 1:9 (TLB) would redirect me: "If you return to me [be willing to receive what I have for you], . . . even though you are exiled to the farthest corners of the universe, I will bring you back to . . . the place . . . I have chosen."

What Gets in the Way: Finding the Link between Past Wounds and Sabotaging Behavior

If receiving results in so many benefits, why is it so difficult for us to do?

Unprocessed shame, feelings of inadequacy, and past trauma make it difficult for us to let down our guard to ask for and receive what we need from others. We're afraid of looking weak. We're afraid of being belittled for needing it. And we're afraid of getting rejected.

Unresolved emotional pain from past trauma develops defenses in our brain to protect us from getting hurt again. These defenses respond automatically to any perception of fear or threat (whether it is true or not) and operate unconsciously like anti-virus software working in the background of our computer's operating system to protect it from malware.

These automatic defenses produce behaviors that sabotage our ability to receive beneficial input from others without us realizing it.

Examples of sabotaging behaviors are:

- disregarding correction to avoid admission of error
- "spinning" everything in our favor to cover feelings of shame
- controlling all the circumstances to prevent dissatisfaction

- dismissing others because their ability threatens our feeling of inadequacy (refer back to: "I Couldn't Receive" in chapter 2)

Having covered ways that sabotage our willingness to receive, let's look at ways to begin allowing the benefits of receiving.

Having an Honest Conversation with Our Emotions

The ability to receive is a function that is already built into our emotional system. We don't have to try harder or be better to do it. Our brain is already wired for it. All we have to do is cooperate with it.

We start by being receptive to ourselves.

Practice being honest about how you feel. You don't have to like or want the feeling. Just practice acknowledging it.

Try relating with your feeling similarly to how you'd relate to a friend. See the emotion. Be there with it. Try having a conversation with the way you feel. Ask the emotion what it is trying to say to you, and then listen. Practice being honest and receiving its response instead of fighting against or trying to bury it.

Some people object to interacting relationally like this with our emotions. They say emotions can't hear and they don't speak audibly. I agree, but I believe they are trying to "tell" us something. So let them do that. Emotions are powerful, and as I mentioned in chapter 1, they are what we experience first in the fast-track of our brain. They will drive our behavior in a sabotaging and unwanted way if we do not become aware of them.

I know this relational concept with our feelings is not a standard way of thinking, but I believe it is possible and helpful to do. The psalmist did something similar when he asked, "Why are you cast down, O my soul?" and then instructed it to "hope in God". (Psalm 42:5 NKJV).

It helps to get more clarity by inviting a trusted, listening friend into the process. Treating your feelings as a personal entity can help you establish a separation between emotional reactions and your true self. I'll say more about discovering that in the next chapter.

Learning to relate to our inner emotional world also helps us learn how to relate more effectively with our outer world—the people we are in relationship with. We develop the capacity to stay in our own discomfort (instead of reacting to it) so we can listen better to the feelings of others. We will grow in the ability to seek understanding instead of defending ourself.

It's this emotional maturity that makes us more attractive and more effective in our relationships.

Receptive Mode

The second way we learn to cooperate with our relationally wired brain is to practice receiving from others.

An unexpected sound in my newly purchased vehicle disappointed me. Service techs said there was nothing wrong with the car, but the subtle whining noise bothered me. I had already paid in full and signed the "no return" paper, so I felt powerless to do anything about it and was desperately afraid I'd be stuck listening to this annoyance for the rest of the car's life.

I became obsessed thinking about it. I'd wake up at night upset and wouldn't be able to go back to sleep. I just *knew* everyone would blow off my complaint and the issue would never get resolved.

And that's when I realized this extreme reaction was coming from some other source than the condition of my automobile.

People say, "don't blame everything on the devil." That's true but the devil's initial work can linger long after he's no longer present. When I was that young boy who felt disregarded about wanting to see Elvis, I bought into the devil's lie that no one cared how I felt. As a result, the wounded part of me went into hiding so it couldn't be exposed to any more rejection. But going into hiding didn't take away the pain and the anger of being disregarded—which is what I was unconsciously reexperiencing with this seemingly hopeless car situation.

It took weeks of conversations, affirmations and suggestions from friends, and prayers with my community to enable me to calm down, separate my reactions from the reality, and see a way forward. I realized I would be more effective at resolving this problem by being relational with the people involved instead of emotionally reacting against them. At the same time, I was encouraged to realize that being honest about my feelings now was reestablishing regard for what that wounded part of me didn't get when I was a boy.

Emotional flare-ups from past unresolved trauma can be the result of believing lies the devil told us a long time ago. When we're younger, inexperienced, and ego-centric, "the father of lies" (John 8:44 ESV) takes advantage of our emotional pain to interject false interpretations about what happened to us. And we believe those false interpretations:

"It's all your fault."
"You're so stupid and hopeless."
"You're not lovable enough to be wanted."

"You can't trust anyone."

"If people knew how bad you are, they would never want to be with you."

These beliefs get so emotionally embedded in our unconscious thinking that they feel normal. Then they become so habituated in our responses that they destructively skew and sabotage our future decisions without us being aware of it.

The only remedy to correct this wrong thinking is to receive love and truth from a community of friends who interact with us tenderly, vulnerably, and honestly.

As of today, I don't know how my vehicle situation will turn out. I do know that my part will be to remain honest and to go about the transaction in a relational way. And I will need the continual support of my friends to give me courage, balance, and appropriateness to do that.

Your effectiveness will depend on that same kind of receiving from others. Slow down. Be in a mode that is willing to listen to both yourself and what others say. Relate honestly with how you feel.

Receiving is the most effective way
to obtain what you want.

Receiving from God

Finally, remember to apply this principle of receiving to your relationship with God. As mentioned earlier in the chapter, receiving from Him is the pathway to obtain a power greater than ourselves and to become something we aren't able to manufacture in our own strength (John 1:12).

As another good friend reminded me about this book: it's creation has been the result of receiving understanding, ideas, and experiences from sources outside of myself.

If you are interested in learning how to receive, consider starting a group to practice it.

· · ·

Startup Guide
for Developing a "Receiving Group"

Begin a conversation about this with a friend.

State the objective: to practice asking for and receiving acceptance, understanding, and whatever you need from another person.

Ask someone if they would be interested in doing this with you.

Find a third person to join you to amplify the satisfying experience.

Establish safety parameters:

- Listen without judgement.
- Don't fix or give advice (unless asked for at the end).
- Be confidential.
- Focus on feelings.

Focus on sharing feelings. Take it slow. Start with something moderate. You could ask each person to relate something they appreciate about another member of the group. You could ask for something positive that someone notices about you or ask for an affirmation and then accept the response. You could ask someone to listen and understand how you feel (without having to agree).

Practice listening to each other. Practice being in a receiving mode. Describe how it feels to be listened to. Describe how it feels to ask for something and to receive what you asked for.

Set an ending date to evaluate the possibility of continuing.

The You You've Always Been
Uncovering the Most Attractive and Effective Part of Yourself

9

AS A KID Jerome was a fun-loving, curious little guy. His adventuresome and enterprising attributes led him to imagine creative ways to achieve his aspirations. He saw no locks or bolts on the doors in his world. And he had the initiative to go after what he wanted. He was also kindhearted, sociable, and naturally trusting of people. But all this changed the night his mother discovered a silver dollar missing from her coin collection, which he had taken to buy something he wanted. The beating he received was so severe, his stepdad had to pull her off of him.

The trauma terrified and confused Jerome. He pulled the covers over his head, sank deep down into his bed, and hid himself away from the world that now felt very overwhelming and unsafe.

As an adult, Jerome holds an influential corporate position with a well-known company. But sometimes this terrifying childhood memory sneaks up on him when he's under pressure, and it can cause him to retreat back into a hiding, protective posture, which covers up the effective attributes of his true self. He has to be very aware that this regression can happen and has to process it with his supportive community so that it doesn't sabotage his potential.

Potential lies within the core of each of us, and it's the most effective part of our true self. It may have been covered up or may never have been realized, but it's there.

God's Word says:

- We are created in His image (Genesis 1:27).
- He has known us before we were conceived (Jeremiah 1:5a).
- He appointed us for a purpose before we were born (Jeremiah 1:5b).

Apart from the redemptive need of our fallen human nature, there is something intrinsic, unique, and intentionally good about each of us that we probably haven't realized. If we allow our true self to be seen and affirmed by others, we will discover our God-given purpose, experience our deepest fulfillment, and make our biggest impact on the world.

This chapter will help you uncover what it takes to develop the most attractive and effective part of yourself.

Your True Self Has Always Existed

The concept of having a preexisting, God-known self with a unique purpose is hard to understand, let alone explain, but consider these verses:

- God "saw me before I was born and scheduled each day of my life before I began to breathe. Every day was recorded in your book" (Psalm 139:16 TLB).
- "O Lord, you have examined my heart and know everything about me. You know when I sit or stand. When far away you know my every thought" (Psalm 139:1–2 TLB).
- "You know what I am going to say before I even say it" (Psalm 139:4 TLB).

- God's choices about us existed "before the foundation of the world" and those choices were "purpose-driven" (Ephesians 1:4 AMP).
- God "has planted eternity [a sense of divine awareness] in the human heart" (Ecclesiastes 3:11 AMP; the bracketed statement is mine).

Many of us find this stuff hard to believe. But it is true!

We are not random, worthless beings with an aimless existence. We have an eternally known and valued part of ourselves, and it has a purpose!

It's one thing to believe it. It's another thing to know how to uncover it. Let's take a look.

The Gold Mine of Our True Self

If you think for a minute about specific passions and values that have always been important to you, you will begin to see attributes of your true self that contain that great potential. No matter how much time passes or how much you have ignored these aspects of who you are, they have never gone away. Examples might include:

- the desire to pursue an out-of-the-ordinary life
- the dream to sing an inspired song to an applauding audience
- the aspiration to hold a certain position in an organization
- the longing to care for children who flock around you
- the yearning to invent something that changes the world

These passions are in there! They're engrained in your true self, and their potential is waiting to be unearthed.

Unconsciously, our true self prompts us to make a stand, work for a cause, or get up in the middle of the night to take action. It expresses itself in activism, a song, poetry, dance, a building we renovate, an article of clothing or jewelry we design. It compels someone to figure out formulas to put people on the moon. It causes some to sit quietly and give a calm presence to the people who enjoy being with them. It produces adorable mannerisms in others that make the rest of us smile.

Our true self expresses itself in uniquely creative ways. And why not!? We are created in the image of One who is uniquely creative.

We discover our true self as we pay attention to our unique attributes and authentically interact in a love-bonded community that affirms, reinforces, and sometimes tenderly redirects us. (More about this later in the chapter.)

Now let's consider ways the realization of our true self gets covered up.

Lack of Validation

When we are emotionally underdeveloped, we're not even aware that a true self exists within us, let alone believe it has worth and potential. We're too busy just trying to survive.

If we are born into an emotionally healthy family, we experience feeling delighted in and valued even when we poop in our diapers or have colicky episodes. We grow up feeling secure enough to explore everything that interests us. When we make mistakes and then find acceptance and encouragement, we're willing to go out and try again. This cycle of exploration allows the uniqueness of our true self to be discovered.

When we don't receive delight and validation growing up, our emotional development stops. We stay stuck trying to satisfy those primary unmet needs, or we dismiss our feelings altogether. When we dismiss our feelings and can't process our emotions, we eliminate the awareness tools necessary for the development of our true self.

The limiting aspects of an emotionally immature adult are:

- a narcissism that dismisses, blames, and resists good advice
- a "victim" mentality to gain sympathy
- joking around to cover pain and discomfort
- pleasing people to get approval
- performing to get recognition
- overachievement to feel worth

Back when I sold furniture, I assumed that factual, stoic presentations would be the most credible way to convey my product to potential architects. I dressed up in a three-piece suit, set my passionate, expressive, true self aside, and acted rigid and unemotional. When my sales manager (who was a good friend and *knew* who I was) accompanied me on one of those occasions, he remarked afterwards, "What were you doing in there? That was awful!"

At the time I was afraid my real self wasn't acceptable, so I tried to be something else to make an impression.

The Stunting Effects of Trauma

There are some things that are so deeply important to each of us that when these values feel disregarded or get intentionally rejected (especially as a tender young child), we hide our true self to prevent that from happening again. (See the discussion in the previous chapter under the subheading "What Gets in the Way.") Sometimes we become an assertive bully to control and hurt others before they control and hurt us.

When we continue acting in ways that protect us from reoccurring trauma, others (and even we) begin to think these behaviors are normal. Eventually people learn to expect us to act like this. But the more unique, authentic, and often sensitive part of our true self gets covered up.

The Condemnation of Shame

Have you noticed how often you feel shame when you try something new, and especially when it fails or when you make a noticeable mistake, however good your intentions were? In his book, *The Soul of Shame*, Curt Thompson writes, "From the beginning it has been God's purpose for this world to be one of emerging goodness, beauty, and joy. [But] Evil has wielded shame as a primary weapon to see to it that that world never happens."[23]

This evil-wielding shame tries to make us feel like we're a bad person for a decision we've sincerely made. It tries to make us feel stupid for expressing ourselves honestly. Experiencing this kind of shame is condemning, and it makes us want to stop expressing ourselves, falsely and profusely apologize to regain favor, and inwardly vow never to try again. It shuts down the development of the most attractive and effective part of our true selves.

But there is something corrective we can do to offset it! Thompson goes on to say, in order to "combat shame" we have to provide "the necessary space for each of us to . . .

grow up to be who we were born to be."[24] Later in the chapter we will return to explain what this "necessary space" is.

Jonah: A Parable of Willful Resistance to His True Self

We can infer from Scripture that Jonah's true self included a supernatural ability to evangelize. When God told him to go to Nineveh and preach, he knew what would happen and refused to do it. There was no way he wanted those cruel, nasty Assyrians to repent and be forgiven by God.

So he ran!

He ran hard and far in the opposite direction, even if it meant drowning in the ocean. But God wanted to use Jonah's ability, so He miraculously saved him with a "great fish" (Jonah 1:17 NKJV) and then delivered him to the destination to accomplish His purpose.

I don't know if it was emotional immaturity that blocked Jonah's acceptance of himself or a traumatic woundedness (perhaps from the Assyrians) that made him so resistant to his calling. But even though a great miracle was performed and 120,000 people were saved, Jonah wasn't able to participate in the joy and satisfaction of being an important part of it. Everything in him resisted who he was called to be, and his life was miserable. He wasn't able to experience how his true self could be so beneficial to others and so fulfilling to himself.

Is there something you are refusing to accept about your true self?

Is there a calling you are running from?

And are you miserable for doing so?

It doesn't have to be that way.

Who you truly are is already eternally known, accepted, and intended by God. Letting yourself express it and letting it develop will be the most effective, satisfying, and God-validating part of your life.

Now let's turn to three ways you can learn to do this.

1. Seeing Yourself through the Eyes of Heaven

You know how good it feels when someone likes you? You can see it on their face and feel it in their smile. It's the most wonderful joy to experience, and it's energizing.

It has taken me decades to understand that God looks at us in the same way. He loves what He sees about our true self and wants to be with us in that. And He wants us to experience the joy of being delighted in by Him.

The problem is, how do we experience feeling loved and wanted when we're so often bogged down with guilt, shame, and negative feelings? The answer: We must receive something from a higher and more loving perspective.

I received God's flooding love as a young man when my former youth leader said a prayer for me. I think he was representing God's perspective of love toward me, and that's what I experienced—even before I had given my heart to Him.

Dr. Karl Lehman coauthored a prayer process called the "Immanuel Approach"[25] that focuses on experiencing interaction with Jesus. This interactive process starts with remembering an appreciation to open the brain's relational circuits and then focuses directly on Jesus to receive His love, joy, and peace about whatever we are going through. The result of experiencing ourselves and our situation through God's restoring and life-giving perspective is always more effective and empowering than trying to talk ourselves into something positive with our own effort.

Mary Anne Quinn, in her ministry Creatively Attached, intentionally applies the Immanuel Approach to build awareness of the person's true identity.[26] Even in older years I still participate in this Immanuel process to continue uncovering the truest version of myself. In a recent session, I envisioned Jesus standing outside the birth canal excitedly waiting for me to be born (see Psalm 71:6). He said He created me to be an adventure and was excited to enjoy this adventure with me. It was like a "restarting experience" in life that made me want to come out and fully engage with Him and everyone else.

The "eyes of heaven" want our true self to be expressed. Romans 5:2 supports this perspective by exhorting us to "look forward to actually becoming all that God has had in mind for us to be" (TLB).

Dr. Lehman says using the Immanuel Approach to experience ourselves being seen through the eyes of heaven works better when we do it in community, which segues into the second way we learn to recognize and develop our true self and its purpose.

2. Seeing Ourselves through the Eyes of Others

In their book about what is so often missing in churches, Jim Wilder and Michel Hendricks wrote, "Perhaps the biggest surprise emerging from brain-scan studies has been that, for our brain, identity develops through attachments."[27]

In other words realizing our unique identity and its potential comes from interactions in affirming, love-bonded relationships—not just by gaining more Bible knowledge.

Neurological experts say we have mirroring neurons in our brain that notice the supporting behavior and the approval of others. We copy what we see other mature and effective people do, and we respond by accepting affirmations about what they enjoy seeing us do.

As Curt Thompson says, "We don't really know ourselves until we see ourselves in someone else's eyes."[28] This relational affirmation is "the necessary space" he was referring to above when he said it is what we need to "grow up to be who we were born to be."

On one public occasion a colleague reminded me to quiet down in consideration of people working in an adjacent room. Even though she conveyed her request in a very kind and considerate way, I was chagrined, once again, and regretted being too passionate and demonstrative when I express myself. When I apologized for being this way, she turned with a heartfelt determination and said to me, "Oh no! That's the best part of you!" I often think back on this affirmation and use it to displace negativity about myself when this shaming part inside me tries to reoccur.

3. Releasing Our Control and Defenses

My wife courageously made the decision to expose her inner struggles to our small group community. Her vulnerability instigated the release of a lifelong bondage to shame that had been covering the sweetness, consideration, and intellectual adeptness that were the attributes of her truest self.

As she let go of her guardedness, the attributes that had always been there and were being affirmed in her became more apparent. I saw a smile when she read a recent encouraging birthday card and heard her say with innocent amazement, "People sure see me differently than I have seen myself!"

Releasing our control and defenses allows others to see and then affirm us for who we truly are.

Connection Revealed My True Self

Recently I woke up with a recurring fear of being too old and too "washed up" to be of any use anymore. It felt like a vicious accusation from someone who was trying to rob me of all the second-chance opportunities I had been hoping for—to gain a healthy do-over in life, to feel specially loved and wanted, to experience one last fruitful episode in life to present what I've learned to the next generation. These despairing feelings were becoming so consistent, I was beginning to fear going to sleep at night.

That's when I remembered to call Lonnie. We had established a close friendship, and both knew that healing comes from heart-to-heart connection and relationships. When I began to share my vulnerable feelings with him, I got nervous and half-expected him to get fed up and start yelling at me to "stop it and grow up."

That didn't happen.

I could almost sense his understanding smile over the phone when he responded, "I've known you for almost sixteen years. I'm pretty aware of your full story, and I know who you are." His implication was, "I'm aware of your emotional 'baggage,' but I know your true self—its strength and its value." He went on to affirm how courageously and maturely he has seen me work through painful issues in the past.

Then I saw it!

From the honest and vulnerable connection with him, I saw the difference between my true self and the insecurity from my childhood attachment pain. And I realized I can remember to draw on the strength of this experience in the future when a part of me feels painfully insecure again.

My maturity keeps growing as I continue to interact authentically with friends and colleagues.

I haven't woken up with those dreadful "washed-up" feelings for a long time.

Live Out of Your True Self

I encourage you to utilize the "eyes of heaven" and the affirming eyes of others to uncover "The You You've Always Been." And then live out of this!

Not only will doing so result in your healing and your life's greatest impact, it will give you the satisfaction and enjoyment of living out of the most attractive and effective part of yourself.

Staying Relational
Even When Life Gets Difficult 10

A MATURE FRIEND related an experience of feeling enraged at his wife. He told her he was so angry he wanted to run away and never come back. He said he wouldn't do that but wanted her to know how upset he was. Throughout this distressing interaction, he stayed calm but remained honest about his feelings. He emotionally connected to her, being considerate of when she became overwhelmed by his feelings. By experiencing him do this, she felt heard and was able to calm down; then both of them processed the situation together and came to a mutual understanding.

In some ways everything in this book points to this desired outcome—staying relational and emotionally available to each other regardless of circumstances in our life.

Staying emotionally available is the key to repairing a relational rupture and ultimately experiencing the most satisfying connection with someone. In any organization it's also the secret to effective customer service and satisfying employee/staff relationships.

And men, listen! Women are specifically attracted to someone who is emotionally available to them. They feel connected to and valued when you do this. My wife conveyed the importance of this during one difficult point in my care giving. She said, "I want you to be present." In other words, *no matter how terrible the situation is or unfixable the problem might seem, I want to experience you in it with me, so I don't feel alone.*

The Art of Being Relationally Angry

In a conference lecture, Pastor Charlotte Lehman framed this concept of staying emotionally available as an important relational "art." She said, "One of the most surprising things I have learned in my twenty-five years of marriage . . . and my . . . years of being lead pastor of our church is that to sustain a joyful community . . . I need to know how to practice 'the art of being relationally angry.'" She further clarified what she meant by saying we need to "learn the skill of staying relational even when we're angry."

That's easier said than done, and Charlotte explained why it doesn't happen: "When people feel angry, they're often instinctively looking for some way to fight back/to feel more powerful/to drown out the emotions of helplessness or fear or shame that are making them feel angry."[29] In other words, they're defensively reacting to the shame of their own insecurity and inadequacy.

I can relate!

It's uncomfortable to feel inadequate, let alone admit it. And lashing out when we feel ashamed like this makes sense, especially to those of us who believe our worth depends on feeling sufficient. But there is a way to emotionally connect with ourselves and another person to process and release these feelings before we act on them. By the way, "lashing out" doesn't always express itself in yelling or attacking; for some "lashing out" demonstrates itself by dismissing the other person and giving them the silent treatment.

But how much healthier and more enjoyable would our relationships be if we could talk about these uncomfortable, shameful emotions so that we could process instead of stuff them, and then experience being listened to and understood.

Talking about Our Upset Feelings

In his book, *You Are the One You've Been Waiting For*, Dr. Richard Schwartz uses the term "courageous love" to describe being willing to communicate our emotions even when we feel afraid, threatened, or ashamed.

Schwartz talks about discerning inner, controlling, managing reactions that don't represent our true self but automatically pop up to protect us from getting hurt. By developing this discernment, he says we can learn to differentiate between our true self and our protective reactions in order to "speak for those powerful feelings rather than being flooded by them and speaking from them."[30] In other words, we can learn to talk about our upset feelings instead of attacking others with them.

Building the emotional capacity to do this can only develop by interacting in relationships. It doesn't happen by our will power or our determination to try harder. Dr. Jim Wilder has often explained that our emotional maturity can only grow by feeling seen and heard in a community and from witnessing others model it who have more maturity than we do.

Allowing ourselves to interact vulnerably in a community starts by giving up our determination to figure it out ourselves. This isn't easy and doesn't come naturally for any of us. But hitting rock bottom in pain and suffering has been a circumstance that has forced me to do it.

I think it's true for all of us.

Pain and Suffering Help Us Get There

It has taken me a long time to admit that pain and suffering are beneficial. I've avoided both for most of my life.

I used to think that devotion was sufficient to motivate me to give up my selfish desires and accept what was best. This sounds noble, but it isn't true. My immaturity and self-focused nature would always take over and drive my behavior the wrong direction. I wouldn't even be able to recognize how detrimental the desires were that I didn't want to give up.

A good Christian friend made the same admission: "I don't have a disciplined prayer time or consistent devoted lifestyle." He said, "I'm more like Jonah. I resist everything God tells me to do at first. I go the opposite direction until uncomfortable circumstances make me turn around. And then I still end up grumbling, even when everything turns out okay."

There is something independent and rebellious about our human and immature nature that wants things the way we want them and convinces ourselves of such even when something deep down tells us it's not right.

That's where the benefit of pain and suffering comes in. It makes us do what we wouldn't do on our own.

I remember exhausting high school football practices. We'd have to do sessions twice a day in the heat of late August to get prepared for the Friday night game as soon as school started. Our uniforms would get so sweat soaked that we'd have to launder them twice a day—after each session. No one liked the exhaustion, but we appreciated what it prepared us for on opening night when the lights came on and all the fans were cheering in the stands.

Evidently the humanity of Jesus needed the same thing because the Bible says Jesus "learned obedience from the things he suffered" (Hebrews 5:8 NLT). Pain and suffering, particularly within our relationships, can have the same beneficial effect on all of us if we let it.

I titled this chapter "Staying Relational: Even When Life Gets Difficult," but the reality is you may not want to be relational *until* life does get difficult. That's how it happened for me.

In the introduction I explained how emotional pain forced me to call someone for help. That was my first step toward emotional development.

Five Benefits of Pain

I know this part might be hard to accept, but I want to encourage you. Below I've listed five ways pain and suffering have helped me (and can help you) develop effective emotional capacity and availability towards others.

1. Pain compels us to take care of ourselves and make gut-wrenching decisions that we previously wouldn't have taken responsibility for.
2. Pain gets us back on the right track. Painful difficulties often get misconstrued as God's unjust treatment. But in the end, after we've surrendered, we see that it had all been meant for the good. The writer of Psalm 119:67 expressed to God: "Before I was afflicted I went astray, but now I keep your word" (ESV).
3. Pain increases our emotional endurance, developing our inner strength and a steadfastness in preparation for even more difficult and important responsibilities in the future (see James 1:4). In Scripture and in history we learn about men and women who were prepared in this way. Joseph was abusively sold and unjustly imprisoned in Egypt to prepare him to lead a country that would save his people from starvation

(Genesis 37–45). Rahab the prostitute accepted her
degrading profession to provide for her family and
in doing so built a faith that not only saved their lives
but positioned her in the lineage of Jesus Christ (see
Joshua 6:25; Matthew 1:5; Hebrews 11:31). Nelson
Mandela was elected president of South Africa after
suffering twenty-seven years behind bars for opposing
its apartheid system.

4. Pain breaks down our defensiveness to allow the
reception of something higher and better.

5. Pain causes us to accept a healthy "shame" about our
behavior that compels us to give in to a correction that
increases our maturity, benefits others, and develops
the best part of ourselves.

In all of these ways pain and suffering have helped me. And
they have especially caused my self-sufficiency to surrender
to this truth that I've known for a long time (but had often
resisted): that my only hope is relying on God, who loves me
relationally and has given promises to save me (see Psalm 25).

And surprisingly, in later years, this surrender (resulting
from pain and suffering) has given me peace and even an unexpected strength and desire to start over to make something
beneficial out of it for others.

Life Is a Relational Journey,
Not a Behavioral Contest

A successful, satisfying life, then, is about emotional connection with others—feeling bonded, understood, appreciated,
and loved. It's not about achieving the most, being right, or
winning an argument.

We're all broken in some area. We all need healing. Our brokenness can't fix itself. We need relational resources outside of ourselves to do that.

John Townsend says we get these resources from one another. He writes in his book *People Fuel*, "We are fuel for each other, great and necessary fuel. And our fueling comes specifically through 'relational nutrients.'" One of John's clients said, "My joy, energy, creativity, career, family relationships, and even my marriage, are all better" because he surrendered his independence and engaged himself in relationships to obtain these nutrients. In his book Dr. Townsend emphasizes, "Longitudinal studies have proven over and over that without significant supportive relationships, we have more psychological dysfunctions, we have more health problems, and we die sooner."[31]

We obtain relational nutrients by sharing our feelings, processing our emotions with one another, and asking for help whenever and wherever we need it.

A Tool to Help Us Obtain Relational Nutrients

Dr. Karl Lehman is a Christian, board-certified psychiatrist who created a "Relational Connection Circuit Checklist" to assess our brain's availability to do this.

In his book, *Outsmarting Yourself*, Dr. Lehman writes,

"Our minds and spirits have been created to *desire* relationship and to *function* best in relationship, and the Lord has actually designed specific circuits in our biological brains to serve this longing and need for connection. When these brain circuits are functioning as designed, our spontaneous, normal experience will be to feel relationally connected and to feel the desire for connection.... We will perceive the presence of others as a source of joy, and we will be glad to be with them.... We will be flexible and creative even when unexpected circumstances require that we change our plans at the last minute.... When these brain circuits are functioning as designed, our spontaneous, normal experience will be to perceive others as allies, *even in difficult interpersonal situations.*"[32]

When this happens, Dr. Lehman says, we will want to join with others in the collaborative process of working together to find a mutually satisfying solution to any problem that arises.

"Unfortunately," he writes, "there are certain problems and conditions that can cause us to temporarily lose access to these brain circuits. When this happens we operate in *non-relational mode* . . . and we won't even want to be connected." He says we won't care how others feel or think and won't be glad to be with them. "Instead of wanting to join, explore, understand, and collaborate we will tend toward judging, interrogating, and focusing on trying to 'fix' the situation." He says that when our relational circuits are off, we will perceive the other person as the problem.

Dr. Lehman emphasizes, "EVERYTHING with respect to relationships will turn out better and flow more easily when you are in relational mode, and operating in relational mode is *especially* important when dealing with conflict."[33]

The following sample of questions are listed in Dr. Lehman's checklist to assess our relational availability:

- Do I feel connected to _____ [fill in name of person involved]?
- Do I feel desire to be connected to _____ [fill in name]?
- Do I experience them as unique, valuable, relational beings?
- Am I aware of their true hearts?
- Do I feel compassionate concern regarding what they are thinking and feeling?
- Am I glad to be with them?
- Am I comfortable making eye contact (other than angry glaring)?
- Can I easily think of things I appreciate about the person, and do I feel gratitude as I think about these specific appreciations?
- Do I experience their presence as a source of joy (as opposed to a problem to be solved or a resource to be used)?

Dr. Lehman says, "If the answers to these questions are 'no,' then your relational connection circuits are off."[34]

In a website essay, Dr. Lehman explained what to do if our relational circuits are off and we want to get them back on:

"Fortunately, the Lord knows that we often lose access to these circuits, and He has provided a plan for getting them back online. He has designed our brains so that perceiving someone with us in our pain, perceiving that this person is glad to be with us, and feeling that this person hears and understands us in our pain will bring our relational connection circuits back online. If there are people in our community who know how to hear us, attune to us, and be with us in this way, then sharing our upset thoughts and emotions with one of these friends can do the job."[35]

This relational circuit checklist is a great tool to use in conversation with someone with whom you want to have a relationship when you realize your own "relational circuits" are off. You could talk about where you are at on the checklist and then ask them to join you, listen, and understand until you feel seen and heard enough to experience a satisfying connection with them.

A New Way to Read 1 Corinthians 13

An important aspect of love is being emotionally available toward the feelings of others and be willing to listen and attune to them. To emphasize this point, I've substituted the phrase "emotionally available" for the word "love" in 1 Corinthian 13. This adaptation is taken from *The Message* version of the Bible.

If I can speak eloquently enough to sweep a woman off her feet and be able to talk someone into doing anything, but am not *emotionally available* to them, I am nothing but an empty, valueless noise.

If I speak God's Word with spiritual giftedness and knowledge and have faith to move mountains but am not *emotionally available* to people, I'm nothing.

If I'm so sold out that I'd give everything I own to the poor and even go to the stake to be burned as a martyr,

but am not *emotionally available* to those around me,
I haven't accomplished a thing. No matter what I say,
what I believe, and what I do, I'm bankrupt without
being *emotionally available* to other people.

Emotional availability never gives up trying.

Emotional availability cares as much about others as it
does myself.

Emotional availability doesn't control and manipulate
to get what it wants.

Emotional availability doesn't have a self-aggrandizing
agenda.

Emotional availability doesn't force itself on others;
isn't about getting what it wants first; doesn't fly off the
handle with anger and rage or pout and feel sorry for
itself when it gets hurt; doesn't keep score when the
other person fails; doesn't revel when the other person
begs and asks for forgiveness.

Emotional availability appreciates when the truth starts
to blossom in another person. It puts up with anything;
trusts God in difficult, painful, seemingly impossible
situations; always looks for the best; never looks back
but keeps going to the end.

The importance of being *emotionally available*
continues to exist for our entire life and for the lives of
everyone around us because our brains were designed

to want and enjoy this connection with each other. Inspired speech will be over some day; praying in tongues will end; understanding will reach its limit. We know only a portion of the truth, and what we understand about God is always incomplete. But when the complete connection with Jesus happens someday, the incomplete stuff in our lives will be canceled.

When I was a young boy, I was only interested in satisfying my own emotional wants and needs. But when I developed the mature ability to be vulnerable and relate as a man, I became more interested in becoming *emotionally available* so I could connect and collaborate with other people in a synchronizing and harmonious way instead of isolating myself and doing everything my way.

We don't yet see things clearly, even when we get older and think we're more experienced and spiritual. We have to give up thinking we're right about everything and give up trying to make everything turn out the way we want it to; instead we need to do something more valuable by emotionally connecting with others.

Being emotionally available offers the most opportunity to experience satisfying and enjoyable connections with each other.

In his book, Dr. Richard Schwartz explains how making our most sensitive and intimate emotional parts available to each other allows this to happen. "Everyone is born with vulnerable parts," he writes. "Those parts are the vulnerability, sensitivity, playfulness, creativity, and spontaneity that are the heart of intimacy"—the parts of us that can experience the most enjoyment with friends and partners. "Most of us, however, learn early—through interactions with caretakers or through traumatic experiences—that being vulnerable is not safe. As a consequence, we lock those [sensitive, intimate] childlike parts away inside and make them the inner exiles of our personalities." Those "heart of intimacy" parts that give the most opportunity for deep, satisfying relationships get buried and are no longer available for connection. (You've encountered people who put up walls and especially men who express tough guy images. They can exhibit physical and spiritual attractiveness, but you can't get close to them. Most of what you experience when you try to connect with them is "anger and cynicism" or a dismissive put-off.)[36]

However, when we honor each other's vulnerability with tenderness, the unguarded spontaneity and playfulness of our true self feels safe enough to express itself and make an enjoyable connection with another person.

Being emotionally available offers the most opportunity to experience satisfying and enjoyable relationships with each other.

Still Mending but Now Together
The Joy and Strength of Emotional Connection

I PUSHED MY WIFE'S WHEELCHAIR into a small lobby adjacent to the coffee shop at the nursing home she was rehabbing in. It was a quiet place to do our daily devotion.

The devotion was about letting God's presence fill our emptiness. While those words sounded good, they didn't do anything to comfort me. And evidently not my wife either.

She recalled attending our enjoyable weekly relationship class, but then regretfully expressed, "When I get home, no one calls me—except the lady who sends a card once a month." With reddened, tearful eyes, she said, "I've always wanted someone to be interested in me." She recounted the time some mission volunteers visited our home a long time ago and intently listened to her talk. She said when they left, she hoped they'd return, but deep down she doubted it would happen and wondered if anyone would ever do that for her again.

It was apparent we were both feeling a similar pain!

Our devotion said to tell God about how we felt, that if we'd make our request known to Him, He would listen. So that's what we did.

It was weeks later, at the end of rehab, when the time came to decide whether my wife should return home. We had previously committed to each other that whatever decision we made, we would make it together. I knew she wanted to come home, and she deserved to. She had worked hard in rehab and had made great progress. But I felt differently. It wasn't a matter of not caring about her. It was a matter of anticipating how overwhelming it would be mentally, emotionally, and physically to be the only one at home to care for her. I knew I'd be lonely, but I felt it would be easier for me (and maybe both of us) if she stayed in the nursing home. My gut ached as I thought about expressing this to her, but not being honest and pretending it would be okay felt like a betrayal of myself that would feel a lot worse.

So I told her I didn't want to do it. She cried and said, "You never could. You've always had a hard time doing something just for me—putting aside what was unpleasant for you just for the sake of doing what I wanted."

It was true. That's how it had been in the past, but my emotional maturity had been developing, and this admission was a part of that growth. I was being authentic, caring for needs I had as well, and knowing that this honesty would be an opportunity for us to create an emotional connection.

And it happened. This time we stayed together in the difficulty. Neither of us shut down. I didn't run. She didn't attack. We didn't revert to self-pity. We just sat there and gave each other the space to feel how difficult and painful it was for both of us. And I'm sure God was answering our earlier prayer with a lot of strengthening grace.

My wife posed a challenging question about how I'd feel in her situation. I agreed that if I was in her position, I would also want to go home. So we considered an alternate plan for her return home that would meet both our needs. The fact that we had learned to stay emotionally connected with each other, instead of defensively reacting, helped us be open to consider this possibility. The story ended well: Social Services helped us find an agency to provide in-home care. Our honesty and attunement to each other's feelings helped both of us establish healthy boundaries and personal responsibilities about her return home.

My wife said this was one of the most difficult but best decisions we'd ever made.

More Healing from Shared Understanding

In the fall of 2022 I attended an experiential workshop at Dennis Del Valle's California Institute of Healing. The workshop was designed to heighten awareness of suppressed emotional pain so that it could be released and healed.

A sense of feeling unwanted and disregarded in childhood came up again. It was hard to substantiate, but it felt real, and I felt angry. Dennis said the look on my face showed I was ready to process something.

He instructed the other participants to role-play what they heard me verbalize. One member played my mom. One played my dad. A couple of them acted out my feelings. One played me as I stood back and watched it unfold.

Getting those feelings off my chest brought some relief, but what gave me deeper satisfaction was realizing that these people understood how I felt and were in it with me. I wasn't alone.

Dennis finished the exercise by having the participants share their experience of role-playing my feelings.

I felt validated and consoled as I experienced them understanding me.

The Effectiveness of Emotional Connection Even in Terrible Situations

What I like best about the concept of emotional connection is that it can be comforting, life-giving, and motivating even in awful circumstances.

I remember a movie about two special forces soldiers jumping out of an airplane and finding themselves trapped in an Afghanistan snowfield surrounded by a Taliban army who opened fire on them. The circumstance was horrible! There was no way of escape. Their commanding officer was irate because he'd been informed that the area was clear. Now there was no way to get the men out, and they were going to die!

I felt despair watching it, but the scene ended with an unspoken sense of triumph, as the commanding officer's surveillance monitor showed two infrared figures stand up to return fire at the enemy and then fall lifeless to the ground.

The men had garnered strength from each other by determining to make one last heroic stand together for a cause they both believed in.

God's Ultimate Desire

Feeling someone want to be with me, listen, and be interested in and attuned to what I'm going through has been one of the most comforting, healing, and enjoyable experiences in my life.

I've now come to believe that God feels the same way; and this is the reason He wants everyone to be saved (1 Timothy 2:4–5 NLT). He wants to be with all of us!

Dr. Karl Lehman, who coauthored *The Immanuel [Prayer] Approach*, writes about this same discovery in his own life.

He explains:

"During most of my years of experience with psychotherapy and emotional healing . . . I saw symptom relief as the primary objective. And then one day I was facilitating a session in which the recipient began to complain about how long the Lord was taking to relieve her pain. She was in a memory where she could perceive the Lord's presence, so I encouraged her to engage directly with Jesus regarding her concern. She expressed her unhappiness directly to Jesus, paused for a couple of minutes, and then reported that the Lord had responded with the following comment: "I love my children, and I am glad to free them from suffering, but the primary, most important purpose of all this emotional healing stuff is to remove the blockages that are between your heart and me."[37]

The most important thing to Jesus is being in a relationship with us!

I eventually realized, "The joy set before Him" that enabled Him to "endure the cross" (Hebrews 12:2 ESV) was exactly that—the anticipation of being with all of us for whom He was dying.

Focusing on experiencing an interactive presence with God is not often emphasized in traditional Christian circles. But there are many references to it throughout the Bible:

- Old Testament examples of God speaking to Moses, Joshua, Gideon, Noah, Debra, the prophets, etc.
- God speaking to Paul, Ananias, Peter, and Phillip in the book of Acts in the Bible.

- References in John 10:16, 25–27 that say, "My sheep hear My voice."

I know it is important to obey God, but in earlier Christian years I lost sight of the initial life-giving and inspiring connection I experienced with God at my conversion. My relationship with God became driven by a legalistic, self-determined effort to stay right with Him by obeying all the rules. It's only in these last few years of experiencing enjoyable connection with others that I've recognized God's identical desire and my longing to reconnect with Him again as my "first love."

In one prayer meeting of regional pastors, I recall a missionary from South America slamming his Bible down on the floor saying, "Brothers, we've made an idol out of this book and what it says instead of relating with and worshipping the Jesus it talks about."

The most important thing to Jesus is being in a relationship with us.

An Update

Today, a year after her last rehab, my wife resides full-time in a nursing home. We also arrived at this decision together, as painful as it was. I felt guilty—even though emotionally and physically drained. My good buddies knew it as well and were heavily involved in listening to and praying for me in the decision. I also understood how my wife felt. She didn't want to give up her home and freedom. But God responded to our urgent prayers. We decided to stop fighting the inevitable decline of our "outward" self and focus on nurturing the inner, relational self that God assures us "is being renewed day by day" (2 Corinthians 4:16 NKJV).

The move worked out well. We have both benefited. She appreciates being cared for by a loving staff, and my visits focus on enjoyable things with her. She listens to and encourages people there as well. They appreciate it and have elected her president of the residential counsel.

Our relationship has grown. In the past we were physically together but emotionally apart. Now we are physically apart but emotionally connecting.

We're both still mending, but tonight when I asked her, my wife nodded in agreement: we are together.

The Challenge and the Results

Men emphasize physical connection but are typically deficient in emotional connection. I certainly was, and I know from interviews with other men that I'm not alone.

At times, I still find myself afraid of being vulnerable, unconsciously seeking refuge in hiding, pretending, or acting "less than." I end up resorting to these behaviors until my community, who values emotional connection as much as I do, reminds me, and it's then I recall how healing and valuable this relational process has been. So I reengage.

A good friend describes the change from my once depressed and despairing demeanor as now being "more buoyant, resilient, and agile emotionally." He said I "roll with the punches instead of getting bogged down in the circumstances."

I attribute this progress to feeling seen, heard, and validated, in vulnerable, emotional connections with others. It's all a part of becoming more attractive and effective.

I wish the same for you!

Endnotes

1. Sharon A. Kuhn, *Empathy: A Guide to Maximizing Human Potential* (self-pub., Sharon A. Kuhn, 2020), 60–61, 78, 80.

2. Marcus Warner and Jim Wilder, *Rare Leadership: 4 Uncommon Habits for Increasing Trust, Joy, and Engagement in the People You Lead* (Chicago, IL: Moody Publishers, 2016), 65–68.

3. Jim Wilder and Marcus Warner, *Rare Leadership in the Workplace* (Chicago, IL: Northfield Publishing, 2021), 8.

4. Warner and Wilder, *Rare Leadership: 4 Uncommon Habits*, 26–31.

5. E. James Wilder III, *The Complete Guide to Living with Men* (Pasadena, CA: Shepherd's House, 2004), 44.

6. Warner and Wilder, *Rare Leadership: 4 Uncommon Habits*, 66.

7. Richard Hostetler, *The Emotional Jesus* (self-pub., Churubusco, IN, 2020), 42.

8. The relationship class used the book by Amy Hamilton Brown, *Journey Groups: Level One: A Relational Discipleship Experience* (Carmel, IN: Deeper Walk International, 2021).

9. Patrick Lencioni, *Getting Naked: A Business Fable...about Shedding the Three Fears that Sabotage Client Loyalty* (San Francisco, CA: Jossey-Bass, 2010), vii–ix, 200.

10. Karl D. Lehman, *The Immanuel Approach: For Emotional Healing and for Life* (Evanston IL: Immanuel Publishing, 2016), chapter 16, "Describe Everything That Comes into Your Awareness," 171–202.

11. Karl Lehman, *Outsmarting Yourself: Catching Your Past Invading the Present and What to Do about It* (Liberty, IL: This JOY! Books, A Division of Three Cord Ministries, 2011), 43–48.

12. Karl Lehman, *Advanced Immanuel Approach Presentation, InterVarsity Staff* Conference 24, Orlando, Florida, January 4, 2024.

13. Adapted from step 2 of *Celebrate Recovery's 12 Steps and Biblical Comparisons*.

14. Henry Cloud, *Cloud-Townsend Resources*, Integrity Outlines, "Establishing and Maintaining Trust," accessed February 24, 2022, www.cloudtownsend.com/trust.

15. Brené Brown, *Atlas of the Heart* (New York, NY: Random House, 2021), 169.

16. Brown, *Atlas of the Heart*, 180.

17. Dr. Vivek Murthy, quoted in Brown, *Atlas of the Heart*, 181.

18. John Cacioppo, quoted in Brown, *Atlas of the Heart*, 179–80.

19. Jonathan Otto and experts and guests, *Autoimmune Secrets LLC*, Gold Series, transcripts of full-length interviews, 2017, 138, 140.

20. Carolyn Carney, *The Power of Group Prayer: How Intercession Transforms Us and the World* (Downers Grove, IL: InterVarsity Press, 2022), 13–16, 40–46.

21. The quotes in this section are from Johann Hari, *Everything You Think You Know about Addiction Is Wrong*, TED Talk, June 2015, https://youtu.be/PY9DcIMGxMs.

22. James G. Friesen, E. James Wilder, Ann M. Bierling, Rick Koepcke, and Maribeth Poole, *Living from the Heart Jesus Gave You* (East Peoria, IL: Shepherd's House, 2016), 36.

23. Curt Thompson, *The Soul of Shame* (Downers Grove, IL, 2015), 13.

24. Thompson, *Soul of Shame*, 13.

25. Karl Lehman, Immanuel Approach.com.

26. Mary Anne Quinn, CreativelyAttached.com.

27. Jim Wilder and Michel Hendricks, *The Other Half of Church* (Chicago, IL: Moody Publishers, 2020), 82.

28. Curt Thompson, "To Know and to Be Known," Biola University Center for Christian Thought, www.youtube.com/watch?v=EMyiuKFElG8.

29. Charlotte Lehman, "On the Art of Being Relationally Angry, Or, 'I Have a Pet Tiger,'" manuscript of a conference lecture, 2016, www.immanuelapproach.com/wp-content/uploads/2020/03/Charlotte-Lehman-On-Anger-I-Have-a-Pet-Tiger-Manuscript.pdf.

30. Richard C. Schwartz, *You Are the One You've Been Waiting For* (Boulder, CO: Sounds True, 2023), 2, 9.
31. John Townsend, *People Fuel* (Grand Rapids, MI: Zondervan, 2019), 28–29.
32. Karl Lehman, *Outsmarting Yourself*, 101–2.
33. Karl Lehman, *Outsmarting Yourself*, 101–2.
34. Karl Lehman, *Outsmarting Yourself*, 119–20.
35. Karl Lehman, "Identifying When You Have Lost Access to Your Relational Connection Circuits, and Getting Them Back Online," essay, originally published July 26, 2008, revised November 12, 2008, PDF, www.kclehman.com/download.php?doc=151.
36. Schwartz, *You Are the One You've Been Waiting For*, 37–38, 43.
37. Karl Lehman, *Immanuel Approach: For Emotional Healing and For Life*, 50–51.

DOUG KELLENBERGER is passionate about helping others realize their full potential and experience more peace and joy through emotional connection. With a master's degree in counseling and a career spanning therapy, seminars, and international sales, Doug offers a unique perspective on how emotions influence the way we relate to God and other people. His writing—whether in his book, blog, or personal communication—explores themes of self-discovery and personal growth, inspiring readers to connect more deeply with themselves and others. Doug is married, has five children and fourteen grandchildren, and enjoys biking, creative communication, and playing bass in his folk bluegrass band.

Stay connected with Doug's latest insights on emotional connection by following his blog:

www.RealMenAreVulnerable.com

Doug is available for podcasts, interviews, speaking engagements, and personal inquiries on emotional connection. He can be reached at **Doug@RealMenAreVulnerable.com.**

Use QR code below to subscribe to his email newsletter and receive his popular free guide: *How to Become More Attractive & Effective: 5 Essential Steps to Emotional Availability.*

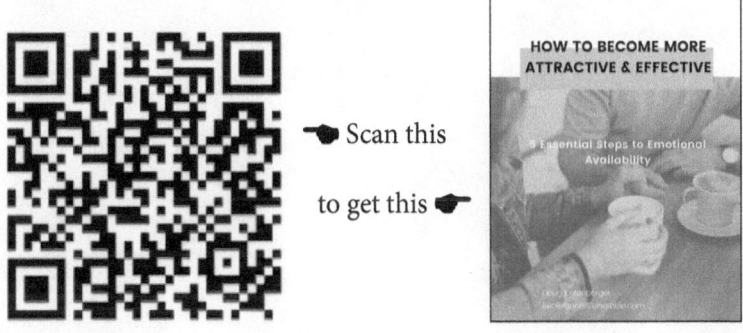

Scan this

to get this ☛

HOW TO BECOME MORE
ATTRACTIVE & EFFECTIVE

5 Essential Steps to Emotional
Availability